(continued)

For volumes in the NCRLL Collection (edited by JoBeth Allen and Donna E. Alvermann) and the Practitioners Bookshelf Series (edited by
Celia Genishi and Donna E. Alvermann), please visit www.tcpress.com.

Reading in a Participatory Culture

Remixing *Moby-Dick* in the English Classroom

EDITED BY

Henry Jenkins and Wyn Kelley

with *Katie Clinton, Jenna McWilliams,*
Ricardo Pitts-Wiley, and Erin Reilly

Teachers College, Columbia University
New York and London

National Writing Project
Berkeley, California

Published simultaneously by Teachers College Press, 1234 Amsterdam Avenue, New York, NY 10027 and National Writing Project, 2105 Bancroft Way, Berkeley, CA 94720-1042

The National Writing Project (NWP) is a nationwide network of educators working together to improve the teaching of writing in the nation's schools and in other settings. NWP provides high-quality professional development programs to teachers in a variety of disciplines and at all levels, from early childhood through university. Through its network of nearly 200 university-based sites, NWP develops the leadership, programs and research needed for teachers to help students become successful writers and learners.

Library of Congress Cataloging-in-Publication Data

Reading in a participatory culture: remixing Moby-Dick in the English classroom / edited by Henry Jenkins and Wyn Kelley ; with Katie Clinton, Jenna McWilliams, Ricardo Pitts-Wiley, and Erin Reilly.
    pages cm. — (Language and literacy series)
Includes bibliographical references and index.
ISBN 978-0-8077-5401-6 (pbk. : alk. paper)
ISBN 978-0-8077-5402-3 (hardcover : alk. paper)
    1. Melville, Herman, 1819–1891. Moby Dick. 2. Melville, Herman, 1819–1891—Study and teaching. 3. Sea stories, American—Study and teaching. 4. Language arts. I. Jenkins, Henry, 1958– editor of compilation. II. Kelley, Wyn, 1951– editor of compilation. III. Clinton, Katie, 1965- editor of compilation. IV. McWilliams, Jenna, 1977- editor of compilation. V. Pitts-Wiley, Ricardo, 1953– editor of compilation. VI. Reilly, Erin, 1972– editor of compilation.
PS2384.M62R42 2013
813'.3—dc23   2012042536

ISBN 978-0-8077-5401-6 (paper)
ISBN 978-0-8077-5402-3 (hardcover)

Printed on acid-free paper
Manufactured in the United States of America

20   19   18   17   16   15   14   13   8   7   6   5   4   3   2   1

Contents

Acknowledgments

The Reading in a Participatory Culture Project was funded by the Digital Media and Learning Initiative of the John D. and Catherine T. MacArthur Foundation. Our work has been consistently inspired by Connie Yowell's vision and determination to create a new field focused on how young people learn in the context of a participatory culture, and we are grateful to Ben Stokes for his critical insights and ongoing engagement with our efforts to model what a more participatory approach to learning might look like.

We want to especially thank the graduate students (Vanessa Bertozzi, Amanda Finkelberg, Neal Grigsby, M. Flourish Klink, Hillary Kolos, Debora Lui, Andres Lombana, Ravi Purushotma, Talieh Rohani, Nick Seaver, Karen Schrier, Stephen Schultze, Parmesh Shahani, and Deja Elana Swartz), researchers (Clement Chau, Russell Francis, and Alice Robison), and staff (Amanda Ford, Jessica Tatlock, Anna Van Someren, Margaret Weigel, Kelly Whitney, and Sarah Wolozin) who helped shape the vision and enable the mission of New Media Literacies during this phase of our research.

We offer a special thanks to Margaret Weigel, whose work with New Media Literacies and with the Strategy Guide provided a strong foundation for the final project.

We are especially thankful for the researchers Daniel T. Hickey and Michelle A. Honeyford, collaborators who were generous with their time, energy, and ideas, and the gifted educators (Lisa Brewster, Paula Browne, Tim Gillis, Jon McDonnell, Judith Nierenberg, Wendy O'Gallagher, Rebecca Rupert, Susan Sylvia, Lynn Sykes, Allison Werlock, and Polly Zajac) who became our key collaborators as we did our initial classroom tests and implementations of these materials.

We also appreciate the rich and wondrous work done by Mixed Magic Theatre (www.mmtri.com), which inspired this project and has continued to renew our excitement about why *Moby-Dick* continues to matter in contemporary culture.

Our thanks go to Howard Gardner, codirector of Project Zero and principal investigator of GoodPlay; Carrie James, GoodPlay research director; the entire GoodPlay team; and GoodPlay research associates Andrea Flores and John Francis.

Preface

One Teacher's Story

Becky Rupert

I was first introduced to New Media Literacies (NML) when Daniel Hickey, a learning sciences professor at Indiana University, stopped by my classroom one afternoon. Daniel asked if I would be interested in testing a new *Teachers' Strategy Guide* (*TSG*) that had been developed by Henry Jenkins and some very smart people from the Massachusetts Institute of Technology. He wondered if I would be willing to work with Michelle Honeyford and an Indiana team to help develop and test assessments for the *TSG*. I said yes, and at that moment, without really knowing what I was in for, I found myself embarking on the most interesting and fulfilling classroom adventure I'd had yet in my teaching career.

When Daniel told me that my kids would be reading *Moby-Dick* as part of the study, I have to be honest—I hesitated. When I told colleagues what my students would be reading, they raised eyebrows, asked me why, and then quickly, nervously wished me good luck. At that time, I taught at a small alternative high school; many of my students were jaded by years of traditional schooling and severely lacking in the academic skills other students their ages take for granted. Many battled to stay awake, focused, and interested, even while reading edgy and relevant young adult fiction that I had handpicked for them. I knew and loved *Moby-Dick*, having read it myself as an undergraduate and then again as a graduate student, but I also knew that it was a big book—a really big book—one full of complexities and allusions to works and worlds my students would not know, full of big words that were going to be unfamiliar, and laden with 19th-century sentence constructions that might overwhelm them. Teaching this book was going to be a big challenge, I thought, and it might take a miracle to pull off. But I had said yes, and I was willing to give it a try.

I didn't count on the intelligence already within that group of students and on their willingness and even eagerness to figure out the complexities together. The *TSG* helped me tap into and enlist their collective intelligence as we discussed the book together. The *TSG*'s first module, "Motives for Reading," asked students to consider their own motives for reading the book, as well as those of their classmates, and even my reasons for teaching it. These differing reasons for reading, reflecting our differing identities, backgrounds, and perspectives, provided multiple lenses through which we could make meaning of the text together. In addition, the *TSG* provided strategies for reading that my students found familiar and even fun and gave me ideas for taking these strategies even further, deepening and expanding my students' understanding of literary texts. Our class became a collective, participatory community deeply engaged in exploring *Moby-Dick*.

The *TSG*'s real beauty is the way its themes and approaches can be remixed and appropriated for other works of literature. In 2009 and 2010, with the help of Daniel Hickey and Jenna McWilliams, an Indiana University graduate student and former NML researcher, I taught the postmodernist text, Tim O'Brien's *The Things They Carried* (1990), using the new media literacy practices of remixing and appropriation (themes found in the second unit in the *TSG*), with equal success. This time, students tweeted in character and created poetry from a collective Twitter feed and then later created fan fiction around specific chapters in *The Things They Carried*. These lessons, though not directly in the *TSG*, were an easy and natural outgrowth of the second unit's principles and themes. In this process, my students developed a deep and personal connection to Tim O'Brien's work, much as we experienced when we read *Moby-Dick* together.

Following our *Moby-Dick* unit, my students and I took a field trip to New Bedford, Massachusetts, where Ishmael and Ahab had embarked on their journey to follow the white whale. I intended the field trip as reinforcement of my students' learning and as a celebration and the culmination of our work together. We wanted to explore the area, go whale watching, and see Ricardo Pitts-Wiley's Mixed Magic Theatre production of *Moby-Dick: Then and Now*, starring Rudy Cabrera—another *TSG* "expert voice." My students were already fans of Rudy, having watched him in several NML videos. We did all those things, but what surprised me more than anything was the very intelligent way my students were able to discuss *Moby-Dick* with experts. In their conversations with MIT Melville scholar Wyn Kelley, Rudy, and Ricardo, my students tapped their own "expert voices" regarding the book. They asked Ricardo intelligent and insightful questions about his choices in writing and staging the play. Their conversation with Wyn in an upper conference room at the New Bedford Whaling Museum further confirmed that my students knew the book through and through. They argued cogently that Melville's chapter "The Town Ho's Story" was an important part of the book, despite the insistence of "experts" that this chapter served little purpose; they argued that this "story within a story" was a sort of foil to the chapter "The Cabin Table" and that both ultimately helped the reader understand the complex social and cultural tensions at play on the *Pequod*. I was a proud teacher sitting at that table as my students talked to Wyn.

My experience using the *TSG* was a huge success. My students' learning far exceeded expectations. In addition to this being a challenging and fun teaching journey for me, I discovered a framework that continues to affect my teaching in surprising and positive ways. I hope that other teachers who bring new media literacy practices into their classrooms have as much success with it as I continue to have.

About the Online Digital Book

Flows of Reading is an online digital book complementary to *Reading in a Participatory Culture*. You can find it at http://scalar.usc.edu/anvc/flowso-freading/index.

This online digital book will introduce and model an expanded concept of "text." While common usage of the word *texts* often refers to written or printed matter, literary and cultural theory extends the term to refer to any coherent set of symbols that transmit meaning to those who know how to read them. In an age where ideas may take many forms, may be expressed across many different media, texts and reading take on new implications. Part of our goal with this project has been to inspire teachers and students, alike, to reflect on what counts as reading and what kinds of reading they perform in their everyday lives. *Flows of Reading* models a new type of reader—one who reads across different media, with reading understood as an activity of sharing, deconstructing, and making meaning.

In *Flows of Reading,* we have organized the material across four intersecting paths. We encourage readers to take ownership of their learning as they select and pursue their own routes through this online digital book. These paths include:

- *Motives for Reading* urges readers to reflect on their own personal motives for approaching a text and to allow themselves to be moved by the flow of others' interpretations and media creations.
- *Appropriation and Remixing* invites readers to apply creative techniques of sampling or combining media that build upon the original texts and move the flow in the direction of new meaning.
- *Negotiating Cultural Spaces* suggests readers examine the social context of unfamiliar texts by purposefully reflecting on the flow of diverse perspectives and behaviors within subcultures.
- *Continuities and Silences* guides readers to explore the associations and absences within texts in order to understand how the flow of meanings converge and get left behind for others to discover.

These four paths offer pedagogical and critical techniques that can be adapted to a range of literary works and offer teachers multiple examples to put these ideas into practice. To ensure versatility of practice, we introduce a variety of texts throughout the paths, such as David Wiesner's *Flotsam* and J. R. R. Tolkien's *Lord of the Rings*.

Our key case study throughout *Flows of Reading* is Herman Melville's *Moby-Dick*, which will enhance the use of this printed book. We share a range of videos, produced by New Media Literacies (NML), including the entire play from Ricardo Pitts-Wiley's *Moby-Dick: Then and Now*. Additionally, we include interviews with our expert voices, further essays which expand on the core concepts from this book, and artifacts showing the classroom application of the *Teachers' Strategy Guide: Reading in a Participatory Culture* (http://www.newmedialiteracies.org/teachers-strategy-guides.php).

NOTE ON THE TEXT OF *MOBY-DICK*

Since *Moby-Dick* is commonly available in many editions, we have used chapter titles and numbers throughout instead of page numbers for our references. But it is important to know that the book appeared in two different first editions (the British and the American) and that many editions collate the two without comment. The one edition that makes the differences visible is the Longman Critical Edition, edited by John Bryant and Haskell Springer, listed in the references.

Part I

FUNDAMENTALS

CHAPTER 1

New Literacies in an Age of Participatory Culture

Katie Clinton, Henry Jenkins,
and Jenna McWilliams

At first glance, playwright, youth organizer, and community activist Ricardo Pitts-Wiley might seem a peculiar inspiration for a book about digital media and participatory culture. Although Pitts-Wiley is enthusiastic about the potential of new media, much of his work is distinctly low-tech. He writes and produces remixed versions of such classics as Herman Melville's *Moby-Dick* and Mary Shelley's *Frankenstein* for a traditional venue: the community stage.

But something magical—something *participatory*—happens on that stage. First, his plays' universal themes are seasoned with immediacy, with issues that resonate with his community. His play *Moby-Dick: Then and Now*, for example, intermingles the themes of Captain Ahab's obsessions, his fatalism, and his willingness to place his crew in peril with contemporary urban gang culture. The whaling trade from Melville's book becomes the drug trade in the contemporary retelling; Ahab becomes Alba, a teenage girl whose brother has been killed by a "WhiteThing" a mysterious figure for the international cocaine cartel; she devotes her life to finding, and killing, those responsible for her brother's death.

In *Moby-Dick: Then and Now*, Pitts-Wiley chose not simply to revise the story, but to incorporate aspects of Melville's version in counterpoint with Alba's quest for vengeance. As the young actors pace the stage, telling their story in contemporary garb, lingo, and swagger, a literal scaffold above their heads holds a second set of actors, who give life to Melville's original tale. The "then" half of the cast is generally older and Whiter than the adolescent, mixed-race "now" actors. The play's meaning lies in the juxtaposition between these two very different worlds, a juxtaposition sometimes showing commonalities, sometimes contrasts.

Reading in a Participatory Culture reflects an equally dramatic meeting between worlds. New Media Literacies (NML) emerged from the MacArthur Foundation's ground-breaking commitment to create a field around digital media and learning. The foundation sought researchers who would investigate how young people learned outside the formal educational setting—through their game play, their fannish participation, "hanging out, messing around, and geeking out" (Ito et al., 2010). The goal was to bring insights drawn from these sites of informal learning to the institutions—schools, museums, and libraries—that affect young people's lives. Right now, many young people are deprived of those most effective learning tools and practices as they step inside the technology-free zone characterizing many schools. Other young people, who lack access to these experiences outside school, are doubly deprived because schools are not helping them to catch up to their more highly connected peers.

New Media Literacies—first at MIT and now at University of Southern California—has brought together a multidisciplinary team of media researchers, designers, and educators to develop new curricular and pedagogical models that could contribute to this larger project. This initiative has been informed by Henry Jenkins's background as a media scholar focused on fan communities and popular culture and by the applied expertise of Erin Reilly, who had previously helped to create Zoey's Room, a widely acclaimed online learning community that employs participatory practices to get young women more engaged with science and technology. The NML team brought together educational researchers (such as Katie Clinton, who studied under James Paul Gee, and Jenna McWilliams, who has an MFA in creative writing and teaching experience in rhetoric and composition) with community-based media literacy veterans (like Anna Van Someren, who ran an afterschool program at the YWCA). Flourish Klink, who had helped to organize the influential Fan Fiction Alley website, which provides beta reading for amateur writers to hone their skills, and Lana Swartz, who had been a classroom teacher working with special need children, also joined the research group. And the development and field testing of curricular resources involved NML in collaborating with other academic researchers, such as scholars engaged in Howard Gardner's GoodPlay Project at Harvard and Dan Hickey, an expert on participatory assessment at Indiana University. NML also worked with youth-focused organizations such as Global Kids, with classroom teachers such as Judith Nierenberg and Lynn Sykes in Massachusetts and Becky Rupert in Indiana—Nierenberg, Sykes, and Rupert were rethinking and reworking *TSG* materials for their instructional purposes—and with scholars such as Wyn Kelley who had long sought new ways to make Melville's works come alive in classrooms around the country.

BETWEEN TWO WORLDS

Popular media representations often set so-called digital literacies at odds with the values and norms of traditional print culture. This book's authors wanted to work across that divide, envisioning a generation of students who could read with a book in one hand and a mouse in the other. In this view, the new media literacies could supplement and expand traditional print literacies in ways that enriched our culture and deepened our appreciation of classical stories. New media platforms and practices were giving students much greater opportunities for communication and expression than could have been imagined by any previous generation. But to participate meaningfully, young people needed to be able to read and write; they needed to know how to connect their contemporary experiences to a much older tradition, and the literature classroom represents a particularly rich environment for fusing these different ways of learning.

Jenkins and Kelley knew when they first met Pitts-Wiley that they had found the perfect co-conspirator on this journey. Pitts-Wiley had gone into an institution for incarcerated youth and helped these young men to learn to read *Moby-Dick* by encouraging them to identify closely with a single character and speculate about what kind of person that character would be if he were living today. In the process, he encouraged them to reimagine *Moby-Dick* as a novel about not the 19th-century whaling trade but rather the 21st-century drug trade—both dangerous professions involving men on the margins of their society who were loyal to each other and to their leaders in their ruthless pursuit of their economic interests.

Pitts-Wiley, in turn, took inspiration from the stories these young men created for his own new stage production, *Moby-Dick: Then and Now*. In the process, Pitts-Wiley became a passionate advocate for getting communities to read and discuss classical novels together. While Pitts-Wiley saw remixing as an important strategy for constructing a productive dialogue with young people around literary works, he was also emphatic that remixing should emerge from a meaningful engagement with the original work. As an African American, he was very aware of how his culture was often "ripped off" by White artists without any acknowledgment of its original meanings and contexts. He asserted his right to draw on the literary canon, but he also insisted that his students pay respect to those who came before. Creative reading worked hand in hand with critical and close reading.

When the Mixed Magic Theatre met NML, the collaboration took all involved outside their comfort zones, forcing each to think more deeply about core assumptions regarding literacy, learning, and cultural expression. Here's how Pitts-Wiley recalls this encounter:

> I didn't feel dumb or unprepared, but I doubted whether I had the language to translate what I was doing into a form that both sides would understand and appreciate. I knew I wasn't up to speed with the technology and concepts the NML team was working with and I wasn't sure they were going to be helpful in putting a play on stage. However, as the work proceeded, both sides realized that it wasn't about allowing technology to dominate. Rather, we were both interested in better understanding how pop culture, access to information, powerful sound, and visuals can hamper or enhance the learning process. I was doing things, as a theater artist, to get my cast to perform with informed honesty, and I came to see that NML was looking for ways to synthesize this process into something that was concise and replicable. As we did so, we were both looking for ways to work around generational, economic, and cultural differences that made the world of MIT and the world my young actors inhabited miles apart.

This book tells the story of what happened when these collaborators sought to bridge these two worlds, what they learned from each other about reading in a participatory culture, how they translated that learning into a framework and a set of classroom activities, and what happened when those approaches got into the hands of gifted teachers. As NML sought to explore how a curriculum for the English language arts classroom could draw upon the mindsets and practices of a participatory culture, it used Herman Melville's *Moby-Dick* as its model text and Pitts-Wiley's play *Moby-Dick: Then and Now* as an example of a contemporary theater adaptation, to develop what NML calls the teachers' strategy guide. The *Teachers' Strategy Guide* (*TSG*) is not simply a lesson plan that tells teachers what to do, but rather represents an approach for teaching literature that embraces and supports participatory practices while foster-ing traditional reading and writing skills.

The *TSG* was field tested in six schools in New England and Indiana, some public, some private; some urban, some rural; some involving high school students, some middle schools; some working with *Moby-Dick*, some adapting the approach to other literary works. Work with the In-diana teachers was overseen by a team of Indiana University educational researchers who were attempting to model new forms of participatory as-sessment. You have already heard from Becky Rupert (see the Preface), one of those educators, and you will get more such perspectives as our account continues. This book will combine some materials drawn from the "Expert Voices" section of our curriculum (New Media Literacies, 2008), essays that introduce our approach and provide some new ways of thinking about what it means to read and write in an evolving media environment, with some assessments of our field testing of this curriculum.

Throughout this book there will be recurring references to *Moby-Dick* to illustrate the NML approach. But you don't need to be teaching this particular book to take advantage of these resources. NML and its collab-orating teachers have adopted this framework to teach a range of other as-signed texts, and Pitts-Wiley has applied the remix practices he developed around the *Moby-Dick* project to other canonical works. So can you. NML's message to educators is simple: Appropriate and remix these practices for your students, apply them to any book you wish or are required to teach, create your own community of readers, and embrace those elements of participatory culture that you think may empower learners.

TOWARD A MORE PARTICIPATORY CULTURE

Over the past several decades, our culture has undergone a period of pro-found and prolonged media change, not simply a shift in the technical in-frastructure for communication but shifts in the cultural logics and social practices that shape the ways we interact. As a society, we are still sort-ing through the long-term implications of these changes. But one thing is clear: These shifts point us toward a more participatory culture, one in which everyday citizens have an expanded capacity to communicate and circulate their ideas, one in which networked communities can help shape our collective agendas. The authors believe that these shifts require us to reimagine the nature of literacy itself.

New Media Literacies (Jenkins et al., 2009, pp. 5–6) defines a participatory culture of the following features:

1. Relatively low barriers to artistic expression and civic engagement;
2. Strong support for creating and sharing creations with others;
3. Some type of informal mentorship whereby what is known by the most experienced is passed along to novices;
4. Members who believe that their contributions matter; and
5. Members who feel some degree of social connection with one another (they care what other people think about what they have created).

Many of the practices of traditional folk cultures embody these same features, with skills and knowledge passed from generation to generation through structures of informal mentorship, mostly involving learning by doing and creating within a shared social context. The institutional and industrialized practices of mass media allow for the mass production and circulation of culture but often at the expense of our abilities to meaningfully participate in those processes at a grassroots level. No longer cultural participants, we have become consumers of culture produced by others and often in the service of their goals, and not our own. Everyday people have lacked access to the infrastructure and resources needed to sustain their own forms of cultural production (Jenkins, 2006a). Digital tools have lowered the costs of production and circulation, decreasing the investment of skills and money required to meaningfully shape our culture, and thus have paved the way for more voices to be heard. In such a world, more and more people have the capacity to take media into their own hands, creating and sharing what they know and how they see the world beyond their immediate friends and families.

And young people are at the heart of these changes. Young people in online forums are engaging in close reading activities directed toward popular music or cult television shows, sometimes engaging in prolonged and impassioned debate about what such works mean and how they convey their meanings; they are recording their impressions, including their reflections on what they read, through blogs, online journals, video reflections, social networks, and microblogging platforms.

In describing steps toward a "more participatory culture," the authors are not asserting that everyone has had an equal chance to participate.

Schools, libraries, and other public institutions have a vital role to play in creating more equitable opportunities for participating. Our students need our help in making sense of a period of profound and prolonged media change that has affected every subject we teach. Ideally, each teacher would take ownership of those new media literacy skills that are part of his or her professional and intellectual domain. The literature teacher, thus, has an obligation to help young people think more deeply about what it means to be a reader and an author in a world where more and more of us can create and circulate what we create with others. To do this, though, we need to negotiate a new stance toward both print and digital culture, embracing new opportunities, even as we preserve older practices, texts, and values.

NML believes that the formal classroom can, should, and must align itself more closely with the clusters of practices that increasingly lead to success in out-of-school environments. Rather than supporting these forms of informal learning, classroom participation structures often minimize opportunities for effective collaboration, participatory engagement with curricular content, and communication practices that extend beyond the physical limits of the schoolhouse. When read through the lens of participatory culture, our formal education system, as it is currently structured, is deeply flawed; these flaws are not apparent through an examination of student test scores, college acceptance rates, or even student satisfaction with their educational experiences. The problem is deeper and much more insidious: The skills, practices, and dispositions students are encouraged to develop are filtered through a system designed for an outdated world. This system, built on a "just-in-case" model of learning (Collins & Halverson, 2009), prepares learners for a life of information consumption but not of active circulation, of critical analysis but not of creative activity (Lankshear & Knobel, 2007).

Clearly, the current U.S. educational system needs radical change. We need to envision an educational system that develops and draws on the diverse talents of all its stakeholders; courts diversity and cultivates creativity and innovation; and takes advantage of the new spaces, tools, and ways of "learning to be" (Brown & Adler, 2008). That said, changes in educational practices are more often evolutionary than revolutionary. There is much that schools and educators can do in the meantime, to make a difference in the lives of their students. And many educators are rising to the challenges of reimagining education for an era of changing opportunities to learn, communicate, and participate in cultural life. As you do so, you may find yourself teaching in new ways, but this transition does not require you to give up on things you value—including books that have been meaningful to previous generations and deep-reading practices that have been productive in helping students understand what they are reading.

Reading in a Participatory Culture offers resources teachers can use in deploying these participatory practices in their classrooms. For us, teaching the new media literacies involves more than simply teaching kids how to use or even to program digital technologies. The new media landscape has as much to do with new social structures and cultural practices as it does with new tools and technologies. And as a consequence, we may be able to teach participatory mindsets and skills even in the absence of rich technological environments. Teaching the new media literacies means helping young people to acquire the habits of mind required to fully engage within a networked public.

DOES LITERACY HAVE A FUTURE?

Reading in a Participatory Culture offers an alternative approach to the many gloom-and-doom books that have depicted the rise of digital expression as a threat to traditional literacies. Nicholas Carr's best-selling book, *The Shallows: What the Internet Is Doing to Our Brains* (2010), offers perhaps the most influential embodiment of contemporary anxieties about the "threat" digital media poses for traditional literacies. Carr sees a "literary ethic" as expressed not only through "what we would normally think of as literature" but also through the work of the historian, the philosopher, and the scientist: "None of these momentous intellectual achievements would have been possible without the changes in reading and writing—and in perceiving and thinking—spurred by the efficient reproduction of long forms on printed pages" (p. 76). Carr worries that the Internet's intellectual ethic creates states of perpetual mental locomotion. This loss of contemplation signals a whole cascade of other losses: "It's not only deep thinking that requires a calm, attentive mind. It's also empathy and compassion" (p. 220). In which case, according to Carr, our uses of digital media are altering the depth not only of our thought but also of our emotions. (For an alternative perspective on how human capacities to communicate have shifted over time see Figure 1.1.)

NML rejects the premise that the new digital mind will render the literary mind obsolete. Rather, the new media literacies build on older print-based literacies, expanding opportunities for human expression, as more and more people pool knowledge and learning together within on-line networks, as teachers expand the learning ecosystem by connecting their students to a larger community of readers, and as writers deploy new media-rich and media-diverse modes of expression and experiment with new literary forms. Our society is at a significant turning point that will redefine how knowledge is produced and stories shared for future genera-tions. What happens in your classrooms is a vital part of the process by which our culture negotiates those changes. The goal should be to embrace those changes that deepen and enrich human consciousness, and to push back on those that trivialize and distract. It would be tragic if we allowed new media literacy practices to totally displace traditional print literacy practices, but refusing to engage with new media out of a misplaced fear of change would be equally tragic.

A well-designed curriculum will help students to develop both the lit-erary mind, as traditionally conceived, and the new competencies required to more meaningfully engage with the new participatory culture. Reading can be both personal and social, both public and private. For this book's authors, deep reading is just one form of a reflective practice. Our expand-ed access to how other people read as we enter digital networks has left us with a deeper appreciation of the breadth of different ways people make meaning from literary texts. Throughout this book, the authors are asking teachers and students to reflect more deeply on their motives for reading, to take greater ownership over the meanings they produce and communi-cate with one another, and to lay claim to certain kinds of expertise that emerge from their unique engagement with shared texts. Contrary to Carr, this book suggests that *deep reading* can be an umbrella term for a whole host of practices, with the goal of readers' finding the particular practices that deepen their engagement with a literary text.

It is problematic to imply that humans could not have "deep thought" or "higher emotions" before the invention of writing, it is simplistic to assume that technologies can support only one mindset, and it is wrong-headed to assume the Internet's intellectual ethic is in direct and total opposition to that associated with books. The history of media change throughout the 20th century suggests that one medium does not displace another, but rather, each adds a new cultural layer, supporting more diverse ways of communicating, thinking, feeling, and creating than existed before. But each new medium also disrupts old patterns, requiring us collectively and individually to actively work through what roles different forms of media are going to play in our lives.

DESIGNING FOR FUTURE LITERACIES

The future of literacy *is* a battleground for what we want and what we need the future to be. We can help to shape the meaning of these new social

Figure 1.1. How Literacies Evolve

Neuroscientist Merlin Donald suggests that the evolution of the human mind is "largely the story of the development of various semantic representational systems" (1991, p. 160), with each new system offering the human mind a new way of representing reality and of generating culture (1993, p. 737). Proposing that humans have passed through three major cognitive transitions, Donald's theory describes how each new form of representation (mimetic, language, external memory) builds on previous forms and arises during a period of rapid, radical change, involving dramatic cultural shifts (1991, p. 16). During the first two transitions—as humans moved from the culture of apes to the culture of *Homo erectus*, and then to the culture of *Homo sapiens*, the major adaptations were biological. The third transition, however, Donald proposes, was technological, whereby new cognitive skills result from the externalization of memory.

Donald suggests that each new skill was layered on the existing set of competencies and practices. In the first transition, humans mastered the expressive potentials of the body-in-motion, adopting mimetic skills, such as the ability to rehearse and refine the body's movements in a voluntary and systematic way, to remember those rehearsals, and to reproduce them on command. These skills, in turn, enabled the development of pre-linguistic symbolic traditions such as rituals, dance, and craft. Next came the emergence of human speech, along with a new cognitive capacity for constructing and decoding narrative (1991, p. 16). The result was an oral culture that supported a much more complex mythology. The next major adaptation involved the development of what Donald calls "external memory," through the written word and, later, through print. During this transition, "thought moves from the relatively informal narrative ramblings of the isolated mind to the collective arena, and ideas thus accumulate over centuries until they acquire the precision of continuously refined exterior devices, of which the prime example is modern science" (p. 16).

Donald argues that

> in principle, this process [of human cognitive evolution] could continue, and we may not yet have seen the final modular configuration of the modern human mind. Theories of human evolution must be expanded and modified to accommodate this possibility. (1991, p. 382)

David Williamson Shaffer and James Kaput (1999) build on Donald's theory by contending that we are currently undergoing a fourth major transition—one based on the ability not simply to store knowledge outside the brain but also to perform new kinds of operations on that knowledge, because of the affordances of digital technologies for externalized processing. We can see and act on the world in new ways as a result of digital modes of representation (e.g., algorithm-based simulations, visualizations): This new system for representing reality enables the development of new ways of meaning—ways that we are only just beginning to explore through our preliminary experiments with these digital affordances.

Donald's stage theory, and Shaffer and Kaput's proposed extension, illustrate how each new form of representation—each new way of representing reality— expands the human cognitive repertoire, even as we preserve and protect the gains of earlier stages in the evolution of human communication. So, mimesis (the body-in-motion as a form of expression) remains a vital mode of communication as deployed in theater and dance, or as captured in the visual arts, and we still rely heavily on gestures and body language in communicating our meaning to each other through face-to-face exchanges. We did not stop speaking once we had the capacity to write, but the functions and status of oral communication shifted as written and printed language could make some tasks easier to perform and allowed knowledge to be more fully exchanged across geographic and temporal distances. Since capacities linked to each previous semantic representational system (mimesis, language) are still with us today, there is no reason to believe that the unique thought patterns and capacities enabled by the technology of writing will be lost. New media have absorbed and enhanced many pre-existing communication capacities, allowing us to deploy sounds and images alongside printed texts, for example, to create a new kind of "writing space" (Bolter, 1991).

Within this new writing space, all previous forms of representation can coexist. And, as it includes wholly new forms of representation, it introduces a new kind of literacy experience. As studied by Clinton (2006, p. 193), a digital technology–based movement (the sort of movement experienced in video games) enables a form of learning-by-being. In games where the player controls the actions of a game character, the process of playing the game (of "reading" the video game) is a process of "writing" the experience of the game character, who could be a specific person (maybe Hamlet, Helen Keller, or a famous peace activist, explorer, or religious figure), a specific *kind* of person (good for teaching disciplinary forms of knowledge [Shaffer, Squire, Halverson, & Gee, 2005], ideologies, and religious perspectives), or even a nonhuman animate form (perhaps a lion, a hawk, or whale). Learning-by-being is similar to the experience of identifying with a character in a book, yet, because of how the process of "being in the gameworld as the game-character" solicits our pre-linguistic sense-making capacities, the feeling of identification is generated at a bodily level. By supporting ways of experiencing stories and data "from the inside," digital technologies open up possibilities for creating literacy experiences that address the problem of student readers' sometimes feeling no affective connections to what they are reading.

practices only if we experience the new modes of action, reflection, and response that they enable. While traditional reading and writing skills remain essential, print-literacy ways of reading, writing, and interacting with text are not enough to satisfy the needs of an increasingly participatory culture.

What follows is a statement of the core principles that guided the design and deployment of the *TSG*. Consider these principles a potential blueprint for other future developments in this space. It is necessarily a statement of values and beliefs, since in designing a curriculum, NML is also laying down stakes for a particular kind of future.

1. Address the Participation Gap

> Access to technology is necessary but not sufficient; all learners must be supported in learning how to contribute, in believing that they can contribute and that what they contribute will be appropriately valued.

The goal of a "participatory" curriculum is to offer strategies for narrowing the participation gap: the unequal access to opportunities, experiences, skills, and knowledge that will prepare youth for full participation in the world of tomorrow (Jenkins et al., 2009). The participation gap is perhaps the most significant and enduring barrier to artistic expression and civic engagement; it is the perception, and often the reality, that even in an increasingly participatory culture not all community members must or even *can* contribute. Technology is pervasive, and young people's access to networked tools is near universal in the United States (Lenhart, Purcell, Smith, & Zickuhr, 2010; Rideout, Foehr, & Roberts, 2010); but that matters very little if many lack the skills required to meaningfully participate or fear that they do not have anything of value to contribute. While some youth are already quite fluent in new media practices, others have had little or no exposure to the "affinity spaces" (Gee, 2004) wherein these new social and cultural skills are being used and, consequently, are at a disadvantage when it comes to knowing how to think and act in a networked society.

Describing a role for schools to help students on both sides of the gap, Jenkins (2007b) notes,

> Even if we see young people acquiring some of these skills on their own, outside of formal educational institutions, there's still a strong role for adults to play in ensuring that young people develop a critical vocabulary for thinking about the place of media in their lives and

engage in meaningful reflection about the ethical choices they make as media producers and participants in online communities." In designing the *TSG*, NML attempted to create a participatory curriculum by harnessing the skills some students already have acquired through new media practices and by expanding access and participation to those who have otherwise been marginalized and excluded from participation.

Key to our efforts to narrow the participation gap is the belief that all writers are also readers and that every reader has the potential to become a writer. Within this model, reading is an essential starting point for creative work. Alongside a notion of reading for mastery, we can add an understanding of reading that crucially links with creative and generative processes that include writing (Brandt, 2009) as well as communication through other genres (video, songwriting, and other forms of expression). Participatory reading is a matter not only of knowing how to respond to a text creatively and critically but also of knowing how to create and circulate content. Proficiency in these practices requires students to define personal motives for reading and to have opportunities for participating in interpretive communities connected to their interests.

Of course, "participation" isn't something that can be taught in a single class or even over the course of a school year. There are many routes to—and diverse forms of—participation, and providing all students the opportunity to develop the knowledge, skills, and dispositions for meaningful participation is a long-term endeavor. Our schools need to make a commitment, at each grade level, and in all subject areas, to support the development of the skills necessary for engaging with the world critically and creatively.

2. Bring New Expertises and Perspectives into the English Language Arts Domain

There are many different forms of literary scholarship, and "literary analysis" is not a monolithic set of practices and skills.

New media technologies make it possible for people to engage with source materials across multiple disciplines and perspectives. In such a culture, meaning-making increasingly extends beyond traditional domain boundaries. How might new voices be brought into the English classroom?

The movement toward multiculturalism has focused on expanding the canon, affecting *what* is read in the English classroom. It is equally important to bring alternative motives for reading into the English classroom in order to expand *how* the canon is read. Bringing new voices (identities, perspectives, expertises) into the English classroom adds new content and introduces new practices. Ideally, doing so also acknowledges how people across fields and domains are working with literary texts in interesting ways, using various media platforms and artifacts; shaping, reshaping, and taking things apart and putting them back together; putting classic texts "in conversation with" contemporary culture.

When we read a text for different reasons in the service of different goals and interests, we read it in different ways, asking different questions, noticing different things, and generating different responses. In school, there has too often been a tendency to reify one kind of reading—one that can easily be reduced to SparkNotes—as if that were the natural or logical way of responding to particular texts. Students are not asked to think about why they, personally, individually, or as members of a larger learning community, might be reading *Moby-Dick*; they have simply been assigned a book, and they are reading it because the teacher, the school board, or the national standards dictate that they should do so. This framing cuts reading in the literature class off from the other reasons young people might choose to read outside the classroom and thus diminishes the relevance of the skills we are teaching.

What if young people were asked to identify their own goals for reading a text, to take responsibility for shaping what they learned from each other, and to translate their engagement with the text into a springboard for other creative, critical, and expressive activities? These questions require teachers to embrace a much more collaborative atmosphere in their classrooms, allowing students to develop and assert distinctive expertise as they pool their knowledge to work through complex problems together.

If literary scholarship is understood as a diverse set of practices, beliefs, and goals, then the notion of reading "as a literary scholar" can be decoupled from generalized expectations about what it means to read. Instead, this approach to reading is understood as being defined by the specific needs of members of a particular discipline, profession, or community. Reading as a literary scholar is certainly valuable, but it is scarcely the only option for a meaningful engagement with a classic text. Indeed, we also find deep value in considering the practices of a broad spectrum of experts and artists as they engage with literary works.

3. Begin with Core Literary Concepts/Practices and Expand

Traditional literacy practices take on new meaning when extended into participatory cultures.

Working from the assumption that traditional literacy practices are necessary, but no longer sufficient, for full social participation in the new digital culture, a strategy for creating activities in the *TSG* was to extend or expand core literary concepts and practices (close reading, allusion, multiculturalism, and structural analysis) to include characteristic "moves" and "moods" of a digital culture. For example, in one early unit, the *TSG* begins with the idea of "close reading," a foundational practice that is traditionally understood as *critical* engagement with a text, and we "expand" this notion to include both the idea of *creative* engagement with a text and a movement from a focus on personal to collective meaning-making. Accordingly, while close reading is traditionally taught as individual engagement with a text, our expanded form of "close reading"—what NML calls "annotation and ornamentation"—suggests that creative reading can work hand in hand with critical reading, and that pooling individual insights can deepen the class's collective comprehension of a text.

Learning to read in this context of shared and dispersed expertise is "messier" than learning to read in a traditional classroom, much as the mixing and matching of production practices within any given creative community is much messier than trying to deal with the practices individually. Teachers reported struggling with their own entrenched assumptions about what forms of culture or what types of reading were valuable and often got caught off guard by materials students wanted to bring into the discussion that had not yet been vetted for their appropriateness or by directions where students wanted to take the conversation that were far removed from the instructor's own expertise and training. Often, students were most engaged when the *TSG* practices felt least like normal schooling and were least engaged when the bureaucratic structures reasserted themselves.

4. Media Studies Approach

Comparative perspectives encourage an exploration of the intersection between literature and other media, often deepening an appreciation of the cultural impact of classic texts.

Students should be taught that a book like *Moby-Dick* is a foundational text that continues to leave its mark on contemporary society. Perhaps the best way to convey this insight is by actively studying the marks that it continues to leave. As *Moby-Dick* is taken up in popular music, film, television, and theater and as the story migrates across space and time, it becomes a site for studying contemporary media practices. Studying these related texts helps students not only to master the text but also to develop a deeper understanding of the contexts through which it circulates, to understand the roles that canonical texts perform in the contemporary media landscape.

Moby-Dick not only is one of the most widely remixed English-language literary texts but also is itself a classic example of a remix. As Kelley points out in Chapter 11 of this book, Melville mixed together travel narratives, scientific treatises, philosophical texts, and myths and Bible stories to craft *Moby-Dick*, and its multigenre characteristics present much of the challenge of reading the book. Since *Moby-Dick* is both a masterful remix and an easy text to repurpose, it makes it an excellent source text for practicing the new media literacy skill of *transmedia navigation*: the ability to follow the flow of stories and information across multiple modalities (Jenkins et al., 2009, p. xiv).

5. Stance on Popular Culture

Popular culture offers a culturally contested and therefore valuable and necessary avenue for developing new media literacies skills.

The *TSG* proposed ways that meaning-making practices developed in the world of popular culture can offer powerful new approaches for reading literature. New media practices represent shifts in the ways we understand ourselves, media, and the world around us; this shift is first enacted in our relations with popular culture, but then the skills we acquire through play are adapted and reapplied and come to have implications for how we learn, work, participate in civic life, and connect with other people around the world (Jenkins, 2006a). People engage with popular culture in part in search of shared and meaningful resources through which they can construct their identities and give expressive shape to their own lived experiences. Bringing such materials and practices into the classroom may give students a chance to reflect more deeply on their own emerging interpretive and creative skills, and deploy them in relation to the kinds of content schools have traditionally promoted.

A core premise of this book is that the English classroom can be a hybrid space in which some pop culture material does have a reason to reside. But doing so means addressing a range of ethical issues that can arise when bringing popular culture content and resources into the English classroom and providing supports and guidance for teachers and students to together negotiate this new ethical territory. Lacking clear guidelines about how to support popular and participatory culture in their classrooms, educators need to proceed at their own risk, a prospect that can be frightening to those used to state-approved curricula and textbooks.

6. Stance on Technology

> There are multiple avenues to participatory culture, and many barriers that limit students' access to these cultures. Our hope is to offer a range of activities, both high- and low-tech, to support as many different kinds of classroom communities as possible.

One aim for creating the *TSG* was to take a first pass at considering how new media practices and mindsets can be applied to reading classic texts. But too many teachers put off introducing new media literacies to their students because they feel that they do not have the right tools and infrastructure to support those digital practices, because they are working with computers clogged with mandatory filters and with policies that block their use of key web 2.0 platforms, because they can't access YouTube or Facebook or Twitter or . . . .

Given the current budget crisis in American education, teachers may be waiting a long time before they achieve those ideal conditions. In the meantime, however, they might introduce *some* of these basic skills and dispositions through offline activities. NML's pedagogical commitment is to create a curriculum that introduces (and offers all students a chance to practice) social and cultural skills valued in a participatory culture, using both online and offline activities. The *TSG*, which offers activities that require minimal access to digital technology in addition to more high-tech approaches to instruction, attempts both to prepare learners for an increasingly participatory, digital future and to acknowledge the realities of our current educational and economic climate—a climate characterized by deep disparities in distribution of technologies and support for their use.

This approach came in handy for Laurel Felt (Jenkins & Felt, 2010), a PhD candidate who joined the NML team after it moved to USC. Laurel found herself teaching the new media literacies in a Senegalese school where the power generator went down at the beginning of the term and stayed down more or less continuously throughout her course. She was able to adopt clotheslines, which are widespread through this community, as a means of identifying and displaying the participatory skills that emerged throughout her interactions with her students.

ABOUT THIS BOOK

Reading in a Participatory Culture is not simply a celebration of an innovative educational experiment: It will also reflect on what went wrong, on some of the ways that schools, students, and teachers struggled to incorporate participatory culture into their pedagogical practices, and on the ways our university-based research team was out of touch with some of the realities that teachers face in the day-to-day practice of schooling in the United States. For example, some of the highest-rated students, those involved in advanced placement classes, were the most impatient with the creative and playful aspects of the curriculum, having already internalized a culture of standardized tests, while other students had difficulty fully grasping what it might mean to embrace a public voice that extended beyond the school itself and to engage others in the larger community. NML also struggled, for example, with filters on school computers that blocked access to *TSG* materials because the title of Herman Melville's literary classic had the word *dick* in it, or principals who were resistant to allowing students to share what they knew on Wikipedia because they had been taught not to trust its contents.

Part I, "Fundamentals," offers an overview of NML, its goals and activities, and the ways it translated a particular understanding of "new media literacies" into a curriculum for teaching canonical literature in the schools. By now, you have already learned about the *TSG* and what NML hoped to achieve by testing this approach through classroom interventions. In the next chapter, you will read more about some of the activities and approaches included in the curriculum and how they emerged from the theoretical commitments described above.

Part II, "Motives for Reading," encourages students to become more familiar with the different kinds of things professionals (literary and media scholars, actors, playwrights, directors) do with classic texts. By examining the process of writing and staging *Moby-Dick: Then and Now* and the trajectories that led participants to their involvement in developing the *TSG*, we share the ways different specialists' reading practices (those of a literary critic, a media scholar, a director/playwright, an actor, etc.) provide a basis for creating different kinds of products (a media analysis, a literary essay, a play, a performance, etc.). Each expert offers an example of how reading is a different kind of thing as it is enacted using different strategies and goals. But why stop there? A more participatory approach to learning demands that students and teacher alike come to grips with their own motives, take ownership of the knowledge they help to generate, and respect the different kinds of expertise that get mobilized through their classroom discussion. Call this situation *co-created learning.*

This unit also links these motives to specific reading practices, making a case for the value of nonlinear reading as a means of extracting meaning from a digressive text like *Moby-Dick.* Drawing on his extensive research into the interpretive communities around fandom, Henry Jenkins explores the diverse ways fans make meaning of the texts that matter to them and then extends this analysis to look at the way Herman Melville represents his own relationship to a community of people invested in whaling within *Moby-Dick.* Wyn Kelley extends this focus on Melville as a reader (who became an author) in her examination of the book's ramshackle structure, its many different goals and the voices through which they are expressed, and the marginal annotations that survive, suggesting the way that the author sought inspiration and critically engaged with a range of different source texts.

Part III, "Learning Through Remixing," digs deeper into the new media literacy skill of appropriation, seeking to understand how a deeper engagement with remix practice might revitalize the study of literature. Many educators confuse the rich forms of appropriation and remixing that characterize participatory culture with the kinds of plagiarism that they have long sought to discourage in their classroom. In practice, remix is much more closely linked to what early literary scholars might have described as "allusions." That is, meaning is created by linking the current text back to earlier works, showing how the author builds upon a larger literary tradition or on the vocabulary of particular genres. Sometimes, the goal is to reference a specific work either to carry forward some of its original meanings or to contest them in ways that may push the cultural conversation to the next level. Henry Jenkins explains the distinctions between artistic debates about appropriation, legal debates about copyright infringement, and ethical debates about plagiarism. Then he offers a series of close readings of how subsequent authors have appropriated and remixed elements from

Moby-Dick in their work, concluding with a consideration of how popular culture references work in Pitts-Wiley's stage play. Wyn Kelley, in turn, examines the processes by which Herman Melville himself created *Moby-Dick* through a similar process of absorbing and remixing elements of the 19th-century whaling culture and previous literary materials and the ways that various characters in the novel model different forms of appropriation as they draw insights from the culture around them.

If *Moby-Dick* can be understood as a series of meaningful fragments, some of which, such as the contents of 19th-century commonplace books, were taken more or less directly from what Melville was reading, the text can also be read in terms of its gaps and silences that have often provided spaces for subsequent readers and authors to insert themselves into the narrative. Wyn Kelley, for example, explores the ways readers are asked to fill in the gaps within what seems at once an exhaustive and elliptical narrative. In particular, she discusses the absence of women in the novel as a challenge that readers, critics, and artists have confronted in various ways. Henry Jenkins, again dipping into the literature on fans and fan fiction, describes some of the properties of texts that have inspired fan authors to write in the margins of existing media narratives, suggesting how teachers might harness this same process to get their students to engage critically and creatively with literary works.

In the final section, Part IV, "Beyond *Moby-Dick*: Challenges and Opportunities," project participants offer reflections about what they learned when NML field tested the *TSG* and the challenges of bringing participatory culture practices and logics into the classroom. NML researcher Hillary Kolos and classroom teacher Judith Nierenberg discuss the ways they adopted the *TSG*'s framework and activities to engage with a young adult novel, *Twists and Turns* (McDonald, 2003), and to help their students develop a richer sense of their own identity as readers and to facilitate new insights into the concept of culture. Jenna McWilliams then describes what happened when a school board decision threatened to close Aurora High School, where Becky Rupert and McWilliams were seeking to expand the *TSG* to provide greater focus on improving students' writing skills. Suddenly, the teacher had a much more applied context that required her to help students improve their communication skills in order to save their school. As McWilliams notes, that initial effort proved unsuccessful in protecting this alternative school from closure and thus raises questions about how the empowerment shaping our concept of participatory culture may or may not prepare students for experiences of disappointment and disillusionment. Learning scientist Daniel Hickey and his collaborators, Michelle Honeyford and Jenna McWilliams, examine the politics of assessment, arguing that our current regimes focused on high-stakes testing often discourage educators from embracing more experimental approaches such as the ones proposed by *Reading in a Participatory Culture.* They propose alternative models for testing participatory learning and illustrate what happened when they adopted these approaches for measuring the success of the Aurora High School students.

In the Conclusion, Katie Clinton and Jenna McWilliams reflect on the tensions encountered in putting some of these ideals about participatory culture into practice within schools as they currently exist. This closing chapter points to the need to negotiate change at the most local level, adopting those practices that can be absorbed by a particular community at a given moment, accepting those conditions that cannot be changed, but continually struggling to transform the nature of schooling as we seek ways to ensure that all students have access to the skills and technologies they need to meaningfully participate in the culture around them.

CHAPTER 2

From Theory to Practice

Building a "Community of Readers" in Your Classroom

Wyn Kelley, Henry Jenkins,
Katie Clinton, and Jenna McWilliams

For students and teachers alike, *Moby-Dick* can seem intimidating at first. Much of its reputation comes from its length and seriousness, but it has also become such an icon, adapted in films and other forms as a weighty tragedy, that many people are surprised to find that it's *fun*: often humorous, full of adventure and odd characters, and refreshingly irreverent about authority and convention. Furthermore, it speaks to young readers expert in using contemporary media. Before you even begin reading the text, you can introduce many key ideas:

1.   Start with the basic premise that there is no better time than now to read *Moby-Dick*. We at last have the tools for tackling a book that many teachers have avoided assigning in the past but that we believe has tremendous power to inspire young readers *today*.

2.   Borrow or buy Sam Ita's *Moby-Dick: A Pop-Up Book* (2007) and let your students examine it closely. This book reproduces many of *Moby-Dick*'s salient features, in terms of not only plot and character but also complexity and beauty. Ask students what they know about *Moby-Dick* before and after reading the pop-up book. What surprises do they find? Explain that Ita's work is "faithful" to Herman Melville's humor, his racial and cultural

diversity, and the intricacy and subtle texturing of his novel, even while using a very different medium.

3. Show a 30- or 60-minute version of Ricardo Pitts-Wiley's play, *Moby-Dick: Then and Now*, and talk about the ways *Moby-Dick* has been adapted in different media and variations over the past 150 years, continually finding new and committed readers. Showing students the way young people have responded to the play makes it clear how powerfully Melville's novel can resonate with contemporary readers.

4. *Moby-Dick* may be a good story that imaginative people might want to make into a pop-up book or a play, but what is the best way to *read* it? Have your students look at Chapter 10, "A Bosom Friend," where Ishmael shows Queequeg, an unlettered Pacific islander, laboriously "reading" a long book by turning and counting the pages. Rather than mock Queequeg's reading practices, Ishmael finds himself moved by them and responds without condescension to Queequeg's idiosyncratic methods. Melville makes the point that sharing a book melts the differences between individuals from worlds completely apart. Students may see a connection between this moment and examples in their own experience of how reading together creates bonds between different people. Reading alone, this scene seems to demonstrate, can be unrewarding; reading with other people in a sociable environment can be a real pleasure.

5. Next, read the Book of Jonah in the Bible and Melville's Chapter 9, "The Sermon," in which Father Mapple fancifully rewrites the biblical story. Have students talk about how Melville shows Father Mapple adapting the text to suit his listeners and his own experiences as a sailor. Discuss how Melville models remixing and appropriation in creative ways.

6. Try showing video clips of this scene from the 1956 movie version of *Moby-Dick* (directed by John Huston), in which Orson Welles plays Mapple, and the 1998 version (directed by Franc Roddam) where Gregory Peck, Huston's Ahab, delivers the sermon. Orson Welles and Gregory Peck in their times were considered actors of the highest authority; directors used them in their films to signal the cultural weight and significance of the book and of these adaptations.

These clips make the point that *Moby-Dick* has had a wide and popular audience in the 20th century, but that serious adaptations have paradoxically led audiences to think that it is a "classic" and hence not accessible to general readers. Point out that *Moby-Dick* was not a classic in Melville's lifetime or for decades thereafter; that, in fact, the movies helped to make it a classic *and* a popular work in the 20th century.

7. Now try reading Melville's first chapter aloud, enjoying the language, Ishmael's delightfully specious arguments about the sea, and his fanlike wonder at the whale.

Such an approach, a sort of browsing through a few of the book's features, should prepare students to expect surprises, think critically about how they read "big books," and anticipate the pleasures ahead. You can, in short, strongly motivate your students to read *Moby-Dick*.

This series of activities, developed by Wyn Kelley, represents a potential starting point for the curriculum described in the *Teachers' Strategy Guide* (*TSG*). Further activities from the *TSG* are included as part of the digital extension of this book. The *TSG* can be understood as an attempt to translate the core insights of the MacArthur-funded Digital Media and Learning Initiative (some of which we identified earlier in this chapter) into an applied context, to suggest ways that teachers could build on this research to change how they teach canonical literature in schools. This chapter will map a few of the links between theory and practice that animated this work, as much to illustrate New Media Literacies' (NML) research process as to make specific recommendations for classroom practice.

MAPPING OUR IDENTITIES AS READERS

In NML's effort to use collective intelligence as an organizing construct for this work, for example, the team developed a trajectory of activities that shifted away from a traditional conceptualization of reading as an individual practice and toward a conception of reading as a collective, and even networked, activity. One of the first activities involved the creation of a Reading Identity Map. Students were asked to take inventory of their own reading practices, inside and outside the classroom. Jenna McWilliams, Katie Clinton, and Debora Lui developed an activity in which young people charted various aspects of their lives and then identified the different kinds of texts they encountered in their daily activities. One Somerville-based teacher, Judi, described how this one activity started to change her students' understanding of reading. One student, for example, had been told for most of her life that she was not a good reader, but through filling out the activity worksheet, she came to realize that "I read all the time."

The Reading Identity Map activity was designed as a prompt for students to gather a sense of themselves as readers and as experts about things that matter to them (getting us away from thinking in terms of abstract categories like "reading comprehension"). The intention was for students to gain a sense of themselves as readers with various and sometimes divergent interests. Then when it came time to read *Moby-Dick*, they would have a better sense of what it might mean for them to explore one aspect of the book (say, a character, a theme, a plot line) that interested them and, through so doing, to develop specialized knowledge that enabled them to make a distinctive contribution to the group's discussion.

An unintended but interesting consequence of this activity was what happened when the teachers also chose to fill out the Reading Identity Maps and to share their maps with their students. Despite students' assumptions to the contrary, teachers are people too—people who read for a range of different purposes and motivations. Students were surprised to see teachers embracing the importance of reading in their lives as parents and grandparents, as hobbyists, as film buffs and music fans. Participating teachers chose to share not only things they know through academic channels but also, like the students, their own personal interests. Students saw their teachers as learners as they pursued these other passions outside school.

This expanded conception of reading thus allows students to understand the reading they do in the classroom as a particular reading practice with its own rules and goals. Rather than judging students' reading practices from the standpoint of a hierarchy, whereby students are taught to devalue the forms of reading that they do in their everyday lives, a participatory understanding of literacy recognizes that there are many ways of making meanings with a text and that all "count" as valid forms of reading.

A COMMUNITY OF READERS

Teachers and students alike were encouraged to think of the classroom as a "community of readers," a metaphor running through Pitts-Wiley's descriptions of his theater practice. He has launched a campaign to get adults to read Melville's novel so that they might engage in meaningful conversations with younger readers in their community. A community of readers offers a supportive environment through which individual students might develop their own expertise and share what they discover about the book and themselves with the group as a whole.

This goal resonated with Lynn Sykes, an English teacher in southern Massachusetts who piloted several collective intelligence-focused classroom activities. Sykes's school had a mandatory silent reading time. Pushing up against the expectation that reading needed to be "silent," Lynn encouraged her students to share what they were reading with one another. They were all reading books of their own choosing (many were reading Stephenie Meyer's *Twilight* series). She also sought to make the school's mandatory reading time fun and social by offering hot chocolate and treats and creating what she called a "Borders Bookstore–like" atmosphere. She saw the collective intelligence activities included in the *TSG*, she said, as new strategies for working toward her goal of creating a community of readers in her classroom.

EXPANDING THE LEARNING ECOLOGY

The school in the digital age is no longer necessarily an isolated location, where learning is cut off from the larger life of the community. Rather, educators can begin to tap into a larger learning ecology, which includes the intellectual resources of parents, community members, and even people who live a great distance from the school. In the case of *Moby-Dick*, the New Bedford Whaling Museum runs a project that links schools along the routes where whalers once traveled, creating opportunities for students to share insights about local history and geography that help them better understand the world Melville depicted in his novel.

An example of a more short-term and powerful connection with an expert occurred in teacher-researcher Becky Rupert's classroom, when students interacted with "post-punk laptop rap" artist MC Lars. Lars is a former English teacher turned "nerdcore" rapper who has released a song, "Ahab," and a music video of the same name. The song is a 3-minute retelling of key themes from *Moby-Dick*, expressed through rap lyrics and in the style of a children's pageant. The *TSG* uses "Ahab" and its video to offer a current and specific example of remix practices related to Melville's novel (see a sample analysis in Chapter 10); students in Rupert's classroom spent several class periods analyzing this remixed text.

As Rupert recognized her students' interest in this video, Henry Jenkins reached out to MC Lars, asking him to participate in an interview project that would enable students to pose questions about his work. Lars agreed, and Rupert's students submitted written and video questions. Lars's answers to these questions were posted online (Jenkins, 2008a). Students saw their words published on a public and popular academic blog, and they followed along as Lars responded, thoughtfully and publicly, to their questions. For some, this was the first time they saw their writing "in public" and as a consequence, some wished they had put greater care into their work. Others felt empowered to participate more fully in other online conversations.

Lars, in turn, was so inspired by even this limited interaction with the students that he has more recently sought ways to more fully engage with NML's work. He is currently teaching an afterschool program at the Robert F. Kennedy School in Los Angeles, where he is helping students to write and perform their own hip-hop songs, inspired by the works of Edgar Allan Poe. Working with the mostly Latino students in his class, he created a music video based on Edgar Allan Poe's "The Masque of the Red Death," which he showcased at a TEDx conference at the University of Southern California. The young, mostly immigrant students saw the story as about class inequalities—the poor die of the plague while the rich party—and constructed a video that personified the Red Death as a force of social justice, warning that "the Red Death will crash your party."

While most teachers don't have direct or consistent access to top scholars or, for that matter, nerdcore performers, most schools are located within networks of experts who can be recruited to engage with young readers. NML's goal here is not to suggest a "career day" for high school students, but instead to suggest that reading, writing, and remixing take on greater relevance when learners can see what these practices look like in professional and amateur communities of readers.

MOBILIZING STUDENT EXPERTISE

The *TSG* sought to encourage students to claim ownership of their own expertise and to share it willingly as part of their roles as members of a community of readers. One way that students came to share their emerging expertise was through the annotation and illumination of Melville's texts.

Wyn Kelley introduced the NML team to the recently recovered marginalia Melville produced as he read books (fiction and nonfiction), which informed his writing of *Moby-Dick* (see Chapter 9). Literary scholars are now exploring how this evidence of Melville's reading might shed light on his creative process. As she did so, NML researchers were struck by how rarely schools encourage students to think about "great authors" as themselves readers of other cultural texts. The *TSG*, on the other hand, saw Melville as a master remixer who took ideas from many sources and mashed them up to create a work that captures the multicultural community that had grown up around whaling.

Having considered Melville's own model, students were then asked to select a page from the novel, blow it up to a poster size, and create their own marginalia. Sometimes, they might write words; other times, they might draw pictures. But they were invited to engage as fully and diversely as possible with what they saw on the page. Because each student brought different motives to his or her reading, each annotation and ornamentation project stressed different aspects. Thus, as they presented the posters to their classmates, many different possible routes of interpretation emerged. In an exchange at "Learning in a Participatory Culture" (one of NML's professional development conferences) in May 2009, Paula—a teacher who had been using the *TSG*—talked about how the classroom dynamic changed within this more participatory model:

> I want to talk about one student's response to the annotation of *Moby-Dick* he did. Afterward, he came to me, and he said, "You know what I figured out from that exercise?" And I'm saying to myself, "Not what the text means, that's for sure." It was really messy, and I didn't come off of it really thinking that they understood all of the text, you know what I mean. They probably couldn't even tell me the plot line. But what he said to me was, "I think what I learned is that I really should read the classics because there's something in there I don't understand," and I thought, Ahh! When you do the traditional way we teach literature to students, somehow the teacher becomes a conduit of all information, no matter how you do it, whether it's a study guide or this and that. Eventually, the teacher tells you how to think about this particular kind of text." What was driving me a little crazy was that I wasn't telling them how to think about anything. The thing I liked was that they came out of it thinking that they better think some more because they really didn't think it through. Eventually, if you are going to be literate,

they have to come to the place where they say that "I had to struggle with this text a little bit to find out what it is saying to me."

Read in this way, the push toward dealing with meaningful chunks from the novel rather than the whole work is not about "lowering expectations" but, rather, about "raising expectations": asking students to engage closely and creatively with specific passages from the text, rather than developing a superficial understanding of the entire work, and asking students to take ownership over what they are learning, rather than relying on the teacher to hand them the answers for the exam. It is about intensive rather than extensive reading. This annotation/ornamentation method of close reading lets each student engage closely with different parts of the story, while benefiting from each other's work.

EXPERIENCING WIKIPEDIA

Schools have often struggled with how to deal with the "Wikipedia problem," seeing student use of the online encyclopedia as something to be discouraged because of the "unreliability" of its means of production. Yet this debate focuses on student consumption of the information already on the site and does not acknowledge that, for those most involved, Wikipedia is a process and not simply a product (Jenkins, 2007a). NML feels that a better approach is one that fosters a deeper understanding of how Wikipedia works, encouraging students to "look under the hood," to see the very transparent operations of the Wikipedia community as it seeks to produce and vet new information—and even to actively participate in reshaping the contents of Wikipedia entries that are relevant to their studies.

One Indiana school encouraged students to make their own contributions to the Wikipedia page focused on *Moby-Dick*. Over the course of the term, their additions faced challenges from others invested in Melville's novels, as is often the case when additions get made to Wikipedia. The students entered into the discussion forum to defend their claims and, in the end, were successful in getting some of their contributions accepted as part of Wikipedia's shared knowledge. As a consequence, the students developed a deeper understanding of research as a process, one that involves an ongoing conversation around what is already known and one that requires different groups of people to bring new perspectives to bear on a shared problem.

STUMP THE EXPERT

For this process to work, teachers need to demystify the concept of expertise. Many students imagine the expert to be someone like the Professor on *Gilligan's Island*, who simply knows everything about everything (except, in that case, how to get off the island), who knows it without needing to check reference books or resources, and who knows it without having to interact with other experts. A much more empowering stance is to recognize many different forms of expertise and to encourage students to identify both what they know better than anyone else and how their knowledge may gain value when placed in dialogue with other kinds of expertise.

In a game NML calls "Stump the Expert," one person in the room—usually the teacher—assumes the role of "expert," choosing a topic about which he or she believes he or she knows a great deal (one teacher we observed chose "dance," for instance). Then, the expert leaves the room and makes a list of everything he or she knows about the topic, while the students are challenged to collaborate on a list of everything *they* know about the same topic, with one or two students serving as the group's scribe. (Participating teachers had success having the students write the list on the board or on a large sheet of paper.)

This activity's goal was not to demonstrate that a group of novices knows more together than a single expert; in fact, the opposite was often true when educators used this game. Sometimes, the expert lists would be thorough and well-organized inventories of general knowledge about an issue; other times, a list would offer a snapshot of the expert's singular and specialized knowledge of the topic.

Even in those cases, however, the students' list would invariably include items not on the expert list. And, in all cases, students had a chance to experience how it feels to contribute what they know, no matter how limited, to a pool of knowledge, often even arguing in defense of including a specific piece of knowledge.

READING ACROSS MEDIA

Kelley's introductory activity was designed to situate *Moby-Dick* not as an abstract text removed from its original media but rather as a work that has changed in dramatic ways as it has moved across different media platforms in the history of its circulation and reception. Rather than seeing these other media versions of the text as distractions from the original, the *TSG* approach sees them as reflections of the living role that canonical literary texts play within contemporary culture. The questions they pose, the stories they tell, and the characters they explore all still speak to current audiences, which is why we continue to read them. As such, educators should be attentive to the processes by which elements of these classic works are appropriated and remixed by a range of other artists.

The *TSG* encouraged students to make cross-media comparisons by exploring how key scenes in *Moby-Dick* are represented in different media forms. Through this process, students come to understand each version as an interpretation of *Moby-Dick*, shaped by constraints of the creator's choice of media format and by the beliefs and values of the cultures in which each creator lives. Students are able to take insights gained through their everyday consumption of popular media as a bridge into the kinds of analytic skills valued in the literary classroom, as they learn to think critically about a range of different kinds of media texts including music videos (*Ahab*), films (several versions of *Moby-Dick*; *Star Trek: The Wrath of Khan*), musical recordings (*Oceana*), and television shows (*Battlestar Galactica*), as well as our central texts—the novel *Moby-Dick* and the stage production *Moby-Dick: Then and Now*. By learning to follow the *Moby-Dick* story as it migrates across multiple media forms (the new media literacy skill NML calls "transmedia navigation") and learning to recognize how creators, working in a range of different media, take elements from *Moby-Dick* and use them as inspiration for their own creative works (the new media literacy skill we call "appropriation"), students are given the chance to develop a familiarity with how a classic text can be made to "speak to" our present realities.

SUPPORTING CREATIVE RESPONSES

We would not consider someone literate by traditional standards if that person could read but did not know how to write. Similarly, media literacy needs to be understood not simply as critical consumption skills but also as skills that expand students' ability to express their ideas across a range of different media platforms and practices. NML tries not to fetishize particular technologies but rather to encourage teachers to provide opportunities for creative and expressive responses to what the class is reading.

As they worked with the *TSG*, different teachers deployed a range of expressive practices to help their students engage more fully with the novels they were reading. Some had students develop comic strips using tools like Bitstrips; some staged and recorded plays much like Pitts-Wiley's own *Moby-Dick: Then and Now*, which emerged from their reinterpretations and appropriations from the novel; some created music videos inspired by MC Lars's *Ahab*, an example that was often incorporated into their teaching of the book; and some had students write fan fiction that explored the perspectives of secondary characters onboard the *Pequod*. The choices of these practices emerged organically from the shifts taking place in the classroom culture, shaped by a changed understanding of the nature of literacy and expertise, informed by the conceptualization of the class as a "community of readers" and their recognition that reading is a springboard for many other kinds of cultural expression.

A *TSG* activity called "Making a Remix" gave students a chance to experiment with different forms of media and explore the kinds *of meaning* they best support. In piloting this activity, NML researchers sent students to a remix site called ccMixter, which features remixes licensed through Creative Commons and makes those remixes available to its community of users. It is perhaps possible to use popular culture resources like ccMixter in a "controlled" way. But any time we introduce a truly networked media resource into the classroom, students are, in a sense, "entering" popular culture, with all its chaos, disruptions, and distractions. As the class explored the ccMixter site, many students gravitated toward sexually explicit and verbally graphic content; they listened to, and in one case transcribed, content that would not normally be encountered in schools. For NML researchers, the ccMixter site came to represent the competing values of defining a more expansive, expressive, and participatory learning community, on the one hand, and protecting children from the (real and perceived) dangers of unregulated communities, on the other.

BRINGING POPULAR CULTURE TO SCHOOL

The *TSG* encouraged participating educators to allow students to mobilize what they knew from informal, outside-school learning contexts, especially those associated with popular and participatory culture, in a classroom setting. We've all seen examples where popular culture was introduced in a jarring way that, in fact, demonstrated the gap between the teacher's culture and those of his or her students: the teacher who brings dated pop records into the class or who tries to speak to the students using slang that is no longer current. The goal should not be to show the teacher's expertise (or lack thereof) within popular culture but rather to allow the students to contribute what they know in ways which are appropriate to the classroom conversation.

A positive example of using a popular culture format in the classroom occurred with the *TSG*'s fan fiction activities. In many English classrooms, students are taught that the most appropriate and sophisticated response to a literary text is a critical essay. In contrast, fan fiction writers use *fiction* to respond to fiction, in the process building communities in which texts are viewed as "open"—as subject to revision, expansion, speculation, and creative elaboration. A main impetus for bringing fan fiction practices into the classroom is to invite students to look at an established literary text as a similar springboard for their own creative inventions.

Fan fiction embodies a particular way of reading the source text (as something that can provoke us to respond) and a particular way of thinking about authorship (as an act of borrowing from and building on what has come before). In fan fiction communities, this notion of accountability to the source text is important. While fan fiction is about getting inside a story and reworking its characters on one's own terms, the act of engaging with a work of fiction creatively is premised on being able to engage with it critically and closely. Although a fan fiction writer is free to engage with the fictional universe of a story in any way he or she wants, fan writers gain credibility for their new interpretations by linking them in meaningful ways to the text and grounding their inventions in specific events or dialogue that shed light on the characters and their motivations.

The idea of accountability to the source text encourages close reading. Equally important is *how* accountability is understood in fan communities: It is not an arbitrary rule, but rather is experienced through the very (consequential) relationship that the fan fiction writer has with his or her readers. The people who read a fan story are reading the fan fiction *because* they are fans of the source text. They care about its fictional universe and often have strong ideas about, and a vested interest in policing, how people use it. Consequently, fan fiction writers look for unrealized potentials in the story (for things to inspire or provoke you to write your own story) but also for elements that other members of their community care about, in order to create a story those readers will accept as a credible interpretation of the source text.

The values and practices of fandom do not directly translate to the English classroom. For one thing, fan fiction writers intentionally speak primarily to readers who already harbor a passion for a work, author, or genre, whereas the English classroom focuses on fostering and supporting that kind of passion. Bringing fan fiction practices into the classroom, however, can create a strong motivation for close reading, as students work from the source text to create their own stories and evaluate their classmates' interpretive fictions.

In this scenario, the community can work together to decide what's "in character" or "out of character" (Black, 2008; Jenkins, 1988), what feels as if it belongs in the fictional world of the original story, and what strays too far from their shared understanding of that world. For example, several classroom discussions focused on speculating on the backstory of Ishmael, the main character of the first several chapters of *Moby-Dick*. In their conversations, students considered reasons why Ishmael would want to go to sea and speculated on his general personality, based on the details Melville provides in the first several chapters of the text. Although students were encouraged to speculate widely, the community returned again and again to the evidence offered in the book. If an interpretation was not supported by details in the novel or was not accurate to the time period, the interpretation was rejected as a scenario that did not "belong" to *Moby-Dick* or its characters.

ACCOMMODATING PARTICIPATION VIA SOCIAL MEDIA

NML researchers had an opportunity to think more about our belief that new media literacy practices can be taught in situations that do not include networked technologies when one of our teachers, Becky Rupert (from Aurora High School in Indiana), created a social network site for her students. This site supported forms of action and interaction that are not easily replicated in offline environments. Working with social networking tools altered the community dynamics—including leading to a shift in who spoke, and about what, and why.

Use of the site, as Rupert explained, had such a transformative effect on her classroom that NML decided to invite students from one of its Massachusetts-based research sites to join their conversation. The hope was to build a geographically distributed community of readers, all focused on the same text, all working together in a shared set of purposes. A series of technical snags made it difficult to create accounts for the students in the Massachusetts classroom; as an interim solution, NML had students log in through an administrator account. On this first day, the team instructed students to "read through the site and the profiles of the Indiana students," telling them that they would have an opportunity to create their own profiles in the next classroom session.

NML researchers should have anticipated what happened next: A small group of students used their anonymity to post comments on the site. The comments were graphic, sometimes sexually explicit, and definitely inappropriate. When Rupert's students logged in the following day, they were welcomed by these comments, which were attributed to the administrator account connected to one team member.

This incident exposed an interesting blind spot: Many adolescents' dispositions toward online social network sites assume a basic right to content creation. The researchers had assumed that students instructed to "read through the site" would do just (and only) that—read through the site. But for the students, the act of reading was automatically connected with their impulse to respond to the site. This incident is a powerful reminder of the will to engage in participatory culture, as well as the challenges of channeling that participation into forms that are meaningful within the classroom.

NOW WHAT?

You will find other examples of how to apply these core concepts in pedagogical practice throughout *Reading in a Participatory Culture* and even more examples within the book's digital extension. Each activity illustrates ways that NML's core commitments can and have been put into action in actual schools. However, NML did not want to produce a formula book of pre-constituted activities. The authors value and respect teachers' own expertise in their subject matter and their students. Thus, we want to encourage teachers to be creative in adapting the models and insights this book contains for use in their own schools, in relation to a much broader range of literary texts and concepts.

This book uses NML's *Moby-Dick* project throughout as an illustration of what is possible, but readers should use this project as an inspiration for developing new approaches to their classroom practice. Some approaches may involve looking at long-used exercises and activities in new ways, and some may involve bringing new technologies and practices into their professional lives. What you choose to bring into the school should be motivated by the content and context you are working with; it should not be seen as a means of entertaining students or holding their attention but rather as a means of respecting their existing expertise and helping them to acquire core skills they will need to meaningfully participate in this new and emerging media landscape.

Part II

MOTIVES FOR READING

CHAPTER 3

Defining Reading

A (Sort of) Historical Perspective

What is reading for? The answer to that question has changed over time and in different cultures. In our discussion of literacy, we recognize that there are many different kinds of literacy, not just in terms of different media but also in terms of the role and function of reading in society. We don't propose new media literacies as a model that can replace one historically limited concept of literacy with another equally limited one. Instead we would like to heighten awareness, in a very general overview, of the many styles and meanings of literacy over time.

MEDIEVAL AND RENAISSANCE MODELS

Literacy did not extend beyond a small class of political, religious, and aristocratic elites before the early modern period in Western history (starting, let's say, with Gutenberg's printing press). Yet within those early elites literacy acquired a range of uses. Laws for church and state had to be written down. Accounts and records had to be kept. Early scientific and historical knowledge could be preserved. Business and personal correspondence facilitated trade, marriage, exploration, political and commercial alliances, and warfare. But what did reading mean beyond these practical uses?

In one early model of writing in medieval Europe monks transcribed religious manuscripts, early scholars read books aloud for pupils or disciples to copy down, or bards produced written texts of oral stories. We might call this model one of *transmission*. From ancient times, humans have recorded their histories, poems, and religious teachings in materials as durable as they could find—stone and wood at first and then the more plastic papyrus, embroidered or woven tapestry, and linen scroll, all long before paper and pen and ink or print (Ong, 2002). This model posits an active giver and a passive receiver. Reading texts allowed one to acquire the wisdom and knowledge of the past. Literacy resided in one's ability to absorb as much as possible of one's heritage; presumably some medieval scholars felt confident of having read *all* known history or religious knowledge.

Another related form of literacy might be thought of as *translation*. Medieval and Renaissance scholars in Europe rediscovered lost archives of books in Latin and Greek. Translating them from Latin, the common language of law, politics, and the church, into vernacular English or French or German made them accessible to a wider range of readers. Shakespeare's early plays depended on, and in effect translated, Latin comedies by Plautus or Italian romances. Shakespeare may have been viewed for a good part of his career less as an imaginative author than as a skillful translator. The Renaissance also saw the rise of vernacular translations of Hebrew and Latin Bibles, and with them an increase in middle-class literacy. With printing available on a broader scale and within a denser urban landscape, more people could enjoy the privileges as well as the pleasures of literacy (Eisenstein, 1979).

ENLIGHTENMENT IDEAS

The European Enlightenment brought ideas of literacy as moral and social *improvement*. In a time when philosophical inquiry spread from the scholarly or monastic cell, penetrating more powerful, concentrated professional and middle classes, and when the middle class competed with older elites for social status, literacy offered both intellectual and practical benefits. John Locke's model of the mind as a tabula rasa, a blank slate (presented in his *An Essay Concerning Human Understanding*), proposed that experiences and texts could write their wisdom on the moral page of the self. Jean-Jacques Rousseau and Benjamin Franklin showed how a guided program of reading the best authors could form an ethical being. In his novel *Emile; or, On Education*, Rousseau offered a model of literacy in which the child absorbs lessons as if from a kindly friend rather than from a stern authority, but the child must still receive these before assuming a place in the adult world. Franklin, in his *Autobiography*, drawing on the precepts of Addison and Steele of the *Spectator,* argued that imitation was the best route to success. One did not read in order to change past models but to acquire their excellences. That one could succeed just as well by imitating the style rather than the substance of one's model lent an ironic subtext to his program.

ROMANTIC NOTIONS

Arising in the revolutionary environment of the late 18th and early 19th centuries, the Romantic concept of literacy posits a radically different view. Religious, political, and patriarchal authority tottered before the vigorous challenges of democratic and working-class ideologies. Secular thinking and a new cult of the individual privileged the power of the self over older forms of sway. Romantic poets and philosophers in Europe and transcendentalists in the United States argued that humans contained a divine spark, an inner authority that could guide them aright. One could read, then, not only to receive the wisdom of the past but also to test one's own character and intelligence, exert one's own will, or experience delight. A book could be thought of as creating a dynamic relationship between author and reader. One could speak of *loving* a book; and in fact sentimental literature, emerging in the mid-18th century under the guise of moral instruction, leapt in the 19th century into full-blown pleasure, entertainment, and titillation. Alarmed parents and pastors issued stern warnings about the dangers of novel reading, especially for impressionable and unprotected youth. Reading at that time might be seen as a form of addiction, when its purposes of cultural transmission, moral instruction, and social improvement were converted to the uses of personal pleasure and choice (Davidson, 1986/2004).

   Romanticism also ennobled writing and reading, lifting them above the practical and moral purposes they had served before and making the writer a Byronic idol, the reader a Poe-ish hero. Since women could now make a living as writers, a number of 19th-century novels—think of Charlotte Brontë's *Jane Eyre* or Susan Warner's *The Wide, Wide World—* applauded women's literacy as leading to happiness, love, and success. Many of our warm and fuzzy feelings about reading derive from the

Romantic notion of literacy as something that makes us better, not necessarily according to some social or ethical standard but simply as a whole and happy being.

VICTORIAN PERSPECTIVES

The Victorians could not always abide such definitions of literacy in a period when Europe was extending its empire over regions it considered backward, primitive, and functionally illiterate. Literacy under empire served to differentiate upright civilization from lazy or vicious barbarism. This period saw the professionalization of letters, as writers of popular and sentimental literature, who had dominated the literary marketplace, ceded their privileged positions, though not their active readerships, to authors considered more weighty, complex, and eventually "modern": authors, that is, who might require an army of critics, professors, and other literary professionals to make sense of their work (Hedrick, 1995). Whereas a typical mid-19th-century book review was nine parts summary, with long excerpts lifted bodily from the text, to one part critical opinion, the 20th century saw the rise of critics who came out of—or more often stayed in—academic enclaves, wrote scholarly monographs, and created elaborate rules by which to evaluate good literature (Lauter, 1994; Renker, 2007). Their arcane terms and discourses would ensure that the world would accord them the same kind of respect it gives to scientists and engineers.

WHAT THESE MODELS SHARE

This idiosyncratic chronology of literacy through the ages is meant more as rough general outline than as a careful history. It is intended to identify different strategies for reading that have appeared at different times in history and that remain in force now. Modern readers still rely on texts for the transmission of knowledge, for translations from other languages, or for enlightenment and improvement. They still conduct romances with books or attack and subdue them for their own profit. They still treat literary scholarship as a science that requires specialized tools and rules and yet they also see reading as the great leveler, the surest sign of democracy in a multicultural society. All these models of reading are still active, and they influence our motives for reading, our practices of reading, and the benefits of reading.

NEW MEDIA LITERACIES

What might be the advantages of thinking about traditional modes of reading in relation to new media? The training students receive in reading is one of our oldest and most powerful experiences, the first mark of a capacity to perform in a literate culture. In the process of learning how to read, every literate person absorbs, at a young age, a broad and potentially confusing range of cultural, ethical, and social lessons. As much as gender, race, religion, class, or national identity, one's literacy defines one's place in society. But like these other givens, literacy need not mean only one thing. Just as one can be male, female, or transgendered, one race or multiracial, a member of more than one religious or ethnic identity, so also one can read in different ways. Why assume that literacy is the simple answer to a complex question?

We take as fundamental the value of broadening and deepening our ideas about literacy by investigating its history, its varying meanings and functions, its different media, forms, and signs. An awareness of the many and surprising paths to literacy can be liberating for students, freeing them to find creative ways to learn and to express what they know, especially in a participatory culture. While there are still gross inequalities in access to digital technologies and associated skills, more and more people have the capacity to take media in their own hands and use powerful new tools to express themselves and to circulate their ideas. In such a world, the borders between reader and writer, consumer and producer, are starting to blur. Young people are at the heart of these changes.

So, what does it mean to teach canonical works at a time when so many young people feel empowered to become authors and to "broadcast" themselves to the world, as YouTube urges its contributors to do? One implication is certainly that they should focus greater attention on what it means to be an author, what it means to be a reader, how the two processes are bound up together, and how authors exist in dialogue with both those who come before and those who follow them. In this context, young people learn how to read in order to know how to create; the works they consume are resources for their own expressive lives. They seek to internalize meanings in order to transform, repurpose, and recirculate them, often in surprising new contexts.

One final point is worth stressing: In this context, literacy is no longer read as a set of personal skills; rather, the new media literacies are a set of social skills and cultural competencies, vitally connected to our increasingly public lives online and to the social networks through which we operate. Just as authors are increasingly seen as sampling and remixing earlier works in their same tradition, so too creative expression, critical engagement, and intellectual argument are understood as part of an exchange that involves multiple minds, and as such, developing literacy is about learning how to read, think, critique, and create together.

This book proceeds with a deep respect for traditional forms of literacy: Without the ability to do close reading or to express one's ideas through written language, none of the other forms of participation we are describing here would be possible. But we also proceed with the understanding that a new cultural context shifts our understanding of the nature of literacy, as it has so many times in the past, and forces people to acquire new skills that were not necessarily part of the curriculum a few decades ago.

Four Readers 1

The Process of Writing *Moby-Dick*: *Then and Now*

Ricardo Pitts-Wiley

My relationship with *Moby-Dick* began when I was a little boy. Whenever the Gregory Peck movie was on television, my mother told a story of when she was in high school in Mississippi. She was very proud of a book report she had written on *Moby-Dick*. But she had to rewrite it after her brother ruined it while shaving. The story and the movie were part of our family lore.

Moby-Dick had always been a part of my life long before I actually sat down and read the full novel. When I read it, it was far better than I could have hoped. It was a struggle getting through it the first time. It was so full of strong images that I had to keep going back. The first thing that impressed me about *Moby-Dick* was the relationship between Queequeg and Ishmael, this male bond that ultimately proved to be very, very important in the novel. I was also struck by Pip from the beginning and by the absolute focus of Ahab. Another part of it that stays with me is Melville's description of the whaling industry and whales. Melville was so obsessed with whales, their scope, their size, their power, their anatomical dimensions. Everything about it was fascinating to me.

BEHIND THE BARS; BETWEEN THE LINES

Fast forward 45 years. After a long career in the theater I began wondering if I could tell *Moby-Dick* as a stage production with a contemporary spin.

As chance would have it, I was asked by AS220, a Providence-based arts organization that had a program in Rhode Island's juvenile detention facility, to cover for a teacher that spring. I told them that my project would be to retell *Moby-Dick* in a manner in which the white whale was a symbol of the cocaine industry. With more than a little trepidation, they agreed. This opportunity would set off a chain of events that would alter the way I approached the theater, literature, and teaching.

From the start of my time with the young men at the training school, I was pleased that my students were willing and eager to read the novel. With so much time on their hands, many of them read a lot. They also read well, remembering details that at times forced me back into the novel. They easily bridged the gap between Melville's time and their own lives. When asked to write and perform a story about a character of their choice, they were able to cut right to the bone.

One of the young men chose Ahab. Ahab was at home, he wrote, back from a very successful voyage of drug dealing for WhiteThing, his boss. He had been so successful that he worried that he was now a threat to the great omnipotent WhiteThing. He realized that it was time for him to either challenge the boss for control or get out of the business. He's home, he's got this young wife, she's pregnant, and the drug lord sends agents looking for him. In looking for him, they kill his wife and unborn child. They don't get him. And now, he seeks revenge for what they did to his family.

Another young man chose Elijah, the prophet with the awful dilemma of being able to see the future and having no one believe or understand what he was trying to relate. His story was about 9/11: "I'm trying to tell you this is going to happen," and then nobody listened. He wrote about how awful Elijah felt that he knew what was going to happen and couldn't stop it.

Another started his story, "I'm Stubb, linebacker, middle linebacker." That just was so right. I mean, you take a character and you sum it up just like that. In the story, Stubb is playing a football game. His girlfriend, a cheerleader, was gunned down on the sideline in a drive-by.

Another young man chose Queequeg, and he made him a pimp. Why a pimp? He explained, "Well, when we meet Queequeg he's selling human heads, shrunken heads, so he's a peddler in human flesh. He's exotic. He's tall. He's good-looking, fiercely loyal, and dangerous. That's a pimp."

The student who chose Ishmael started off by saying, "Ishmael was a Navy SEAL who was so high strung they kicked him out of the U.S. Navy." It's a brilliant description.

Those are just examples. They were extreme, but at the same time the more extreme they got, the closer they got back to the root of the characters. At the end of the process, I worked with the young men to blend their stories into a retelling of *Moby-Dick*. When the young men's stories were combined, all the characters meet at the Spouter Inn to rally around Ahab, who has been wronged. Pip is a soul singer at the inn. Everybody thinks Pip is crazy, but they take him on the voyage because they need levity and entertainment and they recognize that there is a message in his music.

WHAT THEY TAUGHT ME

These young men liberated my thinking. Through their eyes I was able to see Ahab and his crew as ultra human, as people aware of every moment of their lives. I was able to connect with the world that many of my students came from. Theirs was a world that was full of life, color, and excitement. That world was also violent, remorseless, and devoid of discipline. The kids gave me a sense that ultimately *Moby-Dick* is about the nature of revenge and why people seek it. With that kind of insight from them, I was able to go in and fashion a story.

In my actual writing of the play, I didn't use any of these young men's stories, because they belong to their authors. In some ways, even when we cobbled their stories together to make our final presentation, it was a very different kind of story—far more contemporary, far more violent, far less redemptive in many ways, and undoubtedly, far more true than what became *Moby-Dick: Then and Now*. But if you kept looking inside their stories, they were all saying, "Don't ignore me. I can't be forgotten. Listen to me. I do think. I do care about some things," or in some cases, "I have been so stripped of my own humanity. I care about nothing." There was murder in every single one of the stories. There was violence of the highest order. The violence was a natural part of the stories. They justified the violence as being part of the truth of their stories. They were saying, as Melville did, that it is what happens in this world.

Ultimately, when I dealt with a contemporary story based on *Moby-Dick*, I knew that my young crew was not blameless. I felt no obligation to make them into heroes of youth culture. Yes, we want to cheer for them on some level because they're young. But Ahab was in the whaling business, and they were in the drug business. The kids very clearly said, "We're in the drug business. There are occupational risks involved." Perhaps Ahab should have accepted the occupational risks of his own trade.

The kids really freed me up to not see Ahab as a victim or to make the young crew in my adaptation heroes or outside observers of events. But, also, I was able in some ways to free them up to say, "Let's deal with the consequences of our actions. You're already incarcerated so you're dealing with certain consequences of your actions already, but let's deal with the long-term personal responsibility consequences of your actions, and let's deal with the drug and the drug's personality. Let's talk about how many times the drug trade gives you another way out; how little it cares about you on a certain level and also what it gives you." Whale oil lit the world. So does cocaine in a strange way. The kids were making massive amounts of money. Who doesn't want to make money for what they're doing? These questions inspired my own writing process. While the young men were all familiar with drugs, they were not all involved. What I had to come to terms with was the fact that they were the owners of their lives and stories. What I had to honor, above all, was their intelligence and forthrightness in a world that valued neither. I wanted to honor those young men's contributions without appropriating their stories.

They understood Melville's text on a visceral level probably as well as or better than any group that I've ever encountered, including Melville scholars. For example, in the chapter "The Whiteness of the Whale," the whiteness could be read as a symbol of all things good. The students, however, saw Melville as saying, "Don't believe the hype." Moby Dick was White, and, in his quest to live, he killed everything in his path. We were trying to deal with the literary metaphor, and they'd say, "No, the real deal is this. We don't have to coat this or surround this with learned academic insights. Here's the bottom line." That was another way they liberated me. Sometimes I would have to write, "This is the way it is, period. We don't have to sugarcoat it."

The men on the *Pequod* were for the most part the dregs of society. They were a combination of the poor and disposable people. They carried with them a daily expectation of death. They lived a life in violence that they saw as part of the natural order of things. They were also a gang "monkey-roped" to each other; all outsiders were a threat to their safety and well-being. They could read the currents and winds and sense danger. They were dangerous and in danger at the same time. They often responded to and followed the one who was feared the most. They were just like the young men I was teaching.

While the work with the young men at the training school was very important to the writing process, several events further fueled the writing fire. The first occurred in New Bedford, Massachusetts, in the summer of 2005. There was a Melville/Douglass conference going on and I'd been cast to play Babo in a production of Melville's *Benito Cereno*. After the show I met several members of the Melville Society, including Wyn Kelley, a literature professor at MIT. I thought I was fired up about doing an adaptation of *Moby-Dick*. However, their interest, support, and enthusiasm took my enthusiasm to a new level. They had a great passion for Melville's work. As a writer, I remember and respond to things said with a passion. I like to find small passionate things that can connect me to the big story. *Moby-Dick* was a giant story. I knew I had to reduce whole chapters, or whole ideas, to a few lines or an action. Sitting and talking to the Melville Society was akin to listening to true believers recite their favorite verse from the Bible and then express what it meant to them. After meeting them, those things I loved about *Moby-Dick* I loved even more, and they brought me into contact with new things to love.

I remember meeting a Black woman who was at the conference, which surprised me. Although my mother had introduced me to *Moby-Dick*, nothing in my life after that led me to believe that Black people had any interest in the novel. When I saw her, I immediately said, "All right. I want to know why you're here." She spoke eloquently about *Moby-Dick*. She ended our conversation saying, "It's biblical in proportion." Wow, okay, biblical in proportion. Her comment sent me back to the Bible, Shakespeare, and Martin Luther King Jr. and many authors for a joyful reexamination of what that material had to do with Melville's novel.

WORKING WITH THE CAST

The second important event was my encounter with the young people I'd cast in the play. They brought an excitement, intelligence, and energy that was not only a lesson in how to add life to great literature but also a validation of my belief that students of all ages respond best to "in this moment" learning.

Writing for the theater is at best a difficult task. You have to blend language and action, conflict and confusion into characters that an audience can invest in while telling a story that keeps them interested. When you are doing an adaptation of classic literature, you hope all these elements already exist in the original. But the challenge is to see if they can be lifted off the page and maintain some degree of integrity. When spoken aloud, some words that we read and voice with our mind fall flat or have no ring of truth. Some actions that an author may take several pages to describe have to be done in real time.

As a theater artist, the two things I look for in a literary source are clarity of character and action. What's the drama? What's the problem? Drama is always looking for the problem. The problem in *Moby-Dick* is more difficult to find than one might think because the problem isn't really present for so long in the novel. You're 50 pages from the end of the novel before Ahab finds the whale, and it becomes playable on stage. Prior to that, Ahab is just defining the whale and himself, and Ishmael is reporting on Ahab's progress. There's a lot of talking with no action. The crew is not in revolt, although Starbuck is beginning to question some things. It's not until you get into the last chapters of the chase that the conflict is very active. I'm always looking for, Where's the conflict? Where's the problem? And how is the problem going to define the characters?

A novel has the luxury of unfolding slowly. On the stage, as much as playwrights like to resist it, the musical adage "Don't bore us, get to the chorus" is painfully true. I suspect this is also true in teaching young people what is deemed to be a classic work. I feel the student's pain. My desire as a theater artist is to get to the action. While reading *Moby-Dick* I was constantly saying, "Get to the whale. Come on, where's the whale? Get to some action." I had to slow myself down to appreciate the language and the big ideas, the gigantic ideas, the massive ideas that keep giving you something to think about. I pick the novel up all the time, just read my favorite parts, and sometimes I go back and read parts that totally confused me. To me, that's good writing.

Now, I am not one who believes that everything old is good. In fact, I believe that "dominant societies" are inherently in decline because they place a higher value on what has been than on what can be. This may be why so many young people resist classic literature. But I have found that students react differently when those great stories and that great language are lifted off the page and get a new charge. I had to learn to be "in the moment" with my cast every day in the writing and rehearsal process. I had to hear the language for the first time when they heard it. As I became more familiar with the work of New Media Literacies (NML), I came to see that young people were looking for the "close encounters of the first kind" that mashups provide. I had to learn from my cast as I taught them, but always coming back to *Moby-Dick* as the source for that inspiration.

CULLING FROM THE CLASSICS

With *Moby-Dick* I started the story answering the question of why Ahab and Alba, the leader of the young crew, were so angry. In short order I had to get to the "what are we going to do about it?" Okay, we've made our decision; now what are the problems? Melville's work kept saying, Take this idea and say it new. Many times, his language was just right; the way he wrote it was the way to say it, and everyone involved understood that.

The process, nevertheless, always involved culling. The interesting thing about culling is you have to start with something to cull. As a playwright, I often had a strong sense of what was necessary, but it was important to include the cast in the process. I was often surprised at things that they thought were important. I made them fight for every word, but in the end they knew that they had to convey an idea or emotion with 50 words where the author had used an entire chapter.

Each project offers a different set of problems. While it is important to have a focused idea, it is also crucial when young people are involved to let their imaginations fly until they get back to the text, hopefully with a deeper understanding and appreciation for a work that speaks to them and that they can speak to.

You start by asking some pretty basic questions: What is the story? What is the conflict? Who are the characters? What do they say? What do they do? Where does the action take place? What is the arc of time? And on a more personal note: Do you believe strongly that it *is* a story worth telling? Can you, and how do you, maintain respect for the original work while trying to make it immediate and accessible to a contemporary audience? Where are the places where you can take creative and artistic license? Perhaps the most important part of the process, one that served me well again and again was, When in doubt go back to the original text, and don't forget to tell the original author's story first.

Also, if I wish to include elements of hip-hop culture, music, dance, spoken word, mashups, remixes, swagger, and so forth, I have to always keep asking myself why I'm doing it. Can it be done organically? Or am I just trying to fit a square peg into a round hole in an attempt to interact with a young audience?

As much as I was on a journey to understand what Melville was writing about, I also was on a journey to understand hip-hop culture much more specifically. I had two young sons, so I was surrounded by hip-hop.

That doesn't mean that I was a part of it or really understood it—the language and the intent.

The *Pequod* was very much the hip-hop culture 150 years in advance because it was made up of men from multiple cultures that all brought something to the rhythm that was necessary to operate the ship. Their ranks had more to do with skill than with culture or background. The crew members had a core goal, but they all brought their own rhythm and energy to the process. This fusion of the men might have inspired the first mashups. I used Queequeg's funeral to demonstrate this point. Daggoo intoned an African chant, Pip beat his tambourine and sang, and Tashtego sang a Native American song, while the rest of the *Pequod* crew sang "Amazing Grace." While all this was going on, the young crew rapped a tribute to a fallen comrade. In the end, there had to be respect for the traditions that surround dying that Melville had written about.

In creating the crews for *Moby-Dick*, I wanted them to clearly reflect cultures that put something else ahead of race. It was about the *us*. That's why the young crew (the gang) was called "the One." The crew as a whole was more important than any individual. The same was true in the case of the *Pequod*. The crew outweighed individual wants, desires, or needs. Both crews had to have a rhythm—they had to have a way of moving, a way of walking, a way of talking—that defined them even to the point of absurdity.

Well, *Moby-Dick* comes along and never once did that young crew ever discuss race. It never came up. There was a Cambodian crew leader, a Dominican first mate, a White kid, a Black girl from St. Kitts, and a Cape Verdean. They were the crew. They never discussed race, because in that world, it wasn't important. But when it came down to the dancing and the hip-hop, there was a thing that they just all had in common, and they could just go to it, and I loved them for it.

As we moved through the process, I realized also that, in many ways, they had lost touch with where they came from. I'm not so sure that was good, because when I would go to Yosa Yon and say, "Tell me about Cambodia," she could tell me some things, but she didn't really know a lot about it. "Tell me about the Dominican Republic"; Rudy knew quite a bit. But across the board, they didn't necessarily know their own heritage. They had not subverted their culture; they had just relegated it to a place where it didn't have as much impact on their lives. I would often say, "That's important. You don't want to put that on the back burner." The question becomes, How do you balance your past with your future in such a way that you don't repeat the mistakes of your predecessors?

The process of creating and staging *Moby-Dick: Then and Now* provided a great opportunity—on both the upper and lower deck—to show clearly that you can hold on to your identity on a ship or as a nation. But if you don't work together, you die together. In the "Midnight, Forecastle" scene of *Moby-Dick,* all the racial anxiety, hatred, and violence comes to the surface. But then the storm comes up. When the storm comes up, who cares if you don't like me? That's not the issue. I think in many ways the hip-hop culture is saying that the storm is upon us. And we're trying to get ready for it. What are you doing?

ON THE ETHICS OF APPROPRIATION

I'm a product of a Black culture where so much of what we've created has been appropriated and not always for our benefit. The great jazz artists were not necessarily making money off of jazz. The record companies were making money. Our dance forms, our music, our lingo, all of those things have been appropriated many, many times and not typically in a way through which we profited. So when I saw "appropriation" used in relation to new media, I had a lot of concern about it. I still have a lot of concern about it. Does that mean that everything is fair game whether or not you understand its value? Can you just use whatever you want because it's out there? I believe that before you take something and use it, understand it. What does it mean to the people who created it? Where was it born? It doesn't mean that it's not there to be used. It's like music in the air: It's there for everyone to hear it. But don't just assume because you have a computer and can download a Polynesian rhythm and an African rhythm and a Norwegian rhythm that you don't have a responsibility to understand from whence they came; if I'm going to use gospel music I have a responsibility to understand that it's born of a people and a condition that must be acknowledged.

Of course, in writing my adaptation of *Moby-Dick,* it became very important that I didn't appropriate anything that wasn't in the novel from the beginning. People ask me, "Why *Moby-Dick*?" Because everybody was there, so I didn't have to invent any people. On the other hand, I had a real concern about appropriating hip-hop culture and putting it into what we were doing, because I'm not a product of the hip-hop generation. I'm very much an admirer of it. I really had to go to the source and ask the young people, "This is what I'm thinking. Is it appropriate? Is it real? Is it based in any kind of truth, in any kind of reality? What are your thoughts on this?"

If I could make any contribution to the new media literacies, it would be to say to appropriators, "Find the truth. Find the people. Go ask. Go talk to somebody. Do not count on a nonhuman experience in order to make a complete creation of anything."

In remixing I am concerned with questions of who has access and opportunity to appropriate things. If you're media savvy, if you're on the access side of the digital divide, you have access to unlimited knowledge. But does that mean that you know how to use that knowledge and you are respectful of its source?

The first step in remixing novels is to stay honest to the original text, put a value on that, understand it, appreciate it, and then start the remixing process. Edit down to the big questions. Why? What? Why is it important now? And then take the reins off, take the bit out of the mouth, and let imaginations run wild. Imaginations can get very wild and supercreative, so be careful not to censor too harshly or too soon. I value censorship for respect, not necessarily of the original text, but censorship for respect for the reader/participant/audience, so you don't write in a vacuum. I try to write for things to be read and seen. There's great stuff in the original text. Keep going back, and you'll find that those authors really had an idea about what they wanted to write about.

With the work that we're doing at Mixed Magic Theatre, we're not just trying to tell old stories; we're also trying to tell our audience that these stories are a connection to everything. Who's entitled to knowledge? Who feels entitled to culture? From my childhood, I have felt entitled to *Moby-Dick*. For me, staging *Moby-Dick* was about creating conversations between young people and old people, between scholars who often talk only to each other and regular people who often have no access to their ideas. If you finish *Moby-Dick*, you get a key to the *Moby-Dick* village, where there are millions of people from all walks of life. In this village you have something to talk about with everybody.

I believe that Melville is trying to say to his readers, You're entitled to the knowledge of the world. Take advantage of it. I think that's part of what NML is saying. What a glorious concept. Part of my responsibility is telling communities of people who have traditionally been left out that they have to be in the mix. The world's knowledge is there for you. Go and get it.

CHAPTER 5

Four Readers 2

Performing Moby-Dick

Rudy Cabrera

Everything started for me in 11th grade at Central High School with an English teacher by the name of Trish Botkin. She was the first teacher to give me an opportunity to express my love for the culture of hip-hop and to incorporate my knowledge about the inner-city streets into my writing assignments. I remember, when I asked her if my paper could be on the topic of "snitching," she made a statement that still rings in my head to this day: "Rudy, you can write about whatever you'd like; you just have to put it in words I can understand." She told me about Ricardo Pitts-Wiley and his Mixed Magic Theatre company and mentioned how good it would be for me to meet him and get involved with what he was doing. I walked into class one day and here is this stocky bald-headed Black dude with a gray mustache. He looked like the really cool uncle that every family has. After class, we had a chance to speak, and I told him I was interested in acting. He looked at me with a face that made me feel like I was Neo in *The Matrix*. Without using words, he basically told me, If you're going to do this, understand the expectation level and expect a lot of hard work. I was determined and really curious about this whole theater business, so I accepted the invitation.

As I went into my senior year of high school, I met this girl by the name of Yosa Yon (who was later cast as Alba, the modern version of Captain Ahab). I saw her do a monologue in class and was so impressed. I introduced her to Ricardo, and he quickly saw the spark in Yosa. He began telling us about the *Moby-Dick* project. It sounded interesting, and due to my prior experiences with the company, I had to be down. Had I known at the time what it was going to do for me, I would have washed and kissed

Ricardo's feet. We sat down for the reading, and I just remember it was exactly where I needed to be when I needed to be there. I felt so empowered because the young kids' story was an aspect of life I could speak on and know what I'm talking about.

Afterward Ricardo set up a meeting with the young crew to go through the script and update the slang. That day I felt so alive going through the script. I was assisting in making a profound effect with knowledge I was always convinced was useless. For example, "Compared to WhiteThing we just Nemo" was a line I came up with, which people enjoyed and talked about frequently. The witty contrast that line presents I learned from listening to years of hip-hop and watching rap battles. It's something that could easily be flipped into a diss if I say, "When it comes to status you are just below/I'm the big fish in the pond you are just Nemo!"

The acting involved for my character, Que, was very therapeutic for me. He is the direct modern version of Queequeg but also a narrator/philosopher of sorts, so he is also a contemporized Ishmael. The aggression I got to express at moments in the show helped me get a lot of things off my chest. Que wasn't all bad; he was also a writer, a true loyal friend to his crew, a thinker, and at times the only one who really examined and gave a deep analysis to what was going on with the modern story. I often feel that the way many describe Tupac Shakur's role in the movie *Juice* and the way it affected him as a person for the remainder of his life can be applied to my role as Que. In my case, the influence was positive.

The most intimidating thing was getting over the fear of language in *Moby-Dick*. I remember Ricardo saying we had to read the book in order to be in the show. I began reading, and it was so difficult, but being in the show helped. When I got to points that were direct sections used in the show I was thrown back into the story. I learned a lot about the importance of detail through reading and studying *Moby-Dick*. For example, Ricardo explained the importance of the whale facts in the novel; it was to set up just how big Moby Dick really is in comparison with a regular-sized white whale so when he arrives it's clear he's not just any whale.

I can speak for the entire young crew when I say I think we were on the edge the whole way through script development, rehearsals, and performances because we were also responsible for bringing knowledge to the table. This was not a project where the modern story and the original one were dealt with separately. We were put on the spot plenty of times. We were expected to understand not just what we knew about the modern world and how our lives pertain to "the One" but also the older world and what Herman

Melville was really trying to tell us using the *Pequod*. That connected the entire project. There was rarely a rehearsal where only the adults or only the youth were called in. We were there as one all the way through learning from each other. The adults would comment on things with "the One," and the kids would comment on things with "the *Pequod*." It was a melting pot that made everyone important and valuable. If every kid could have an experience like this we'd be living in an entirely different world.

"Do not talk to me of blasphemy, man. I'd strike the sun if it insulted me" was and still is my favorite line in the whole play. At the time I would hear that line and get chills and think to myself, "Ahab is a G, he's straight-up gangster," but now I have a different outlook on life, although I still love the line. I understand that my enjoyment of it has to be handled with great care when presenting it to younger kids who come from the same background as mine and value the same things I once valued. What people have to understand is that Ahab's relentlessness was not noble and was not something anyone should look up to. Ahab was selfish and hardheaded and took down an entire ship of people because he made Moby Dick a personal issue in his own head. It became most important for us as the young crew to understand that Captain Ahab's anger toward Moby Dick was completely uncalled for and unjust because he was in the whale's path. This lesson was big and is completely relevant not only to myself and the young crew but also to the kids in the streets every day. It has to be handled very carefully because Captain Ahab can easily become a young kid's favorite character for all the wrong reasons. Captain Ahab thought he could kill Moby Dick. The only way Ahab was going to win was to stay out of Moby Dick's way. Alba and the young crew learned the same lesson about WhiteThing (the contemporized version of Moby Dick representing the entire cocaine trade business) before it was too late. In the end it's about what happens when you follow bad leaders (a big lesson I had to acquire personally and apply later on in my life). In studying the other members of the *Pequod*, I learned that you have to be careful about whom you give your loyalty to because someone who isn't clear-headed enough to be invested in his or her own well-being will not handle your life with care.

It was almost surreal performing in *Moby-Dick,* especially once MIT and the New Media Literacies (NML) project came into the picture. Probably most significant was that my opinion or point of view became valuable. The really interesting part about it though was the fact that once I began doing the interviews for the project and speaking with people like Wyn

Kelley, whatever insecurities I had were immediately gone. I just spoke from the heart about what I had been experiencing and didn't think of it as interesting until I went back and watched the footage. I would see myself speaking on camera but almost couldn't believe it was me; I would hear myself say certain things, and I had to fully digest them because they were actually interesting ideas.

As I examine my life before *Moby-Dick* I remember a story that almost kept me from being involved with Mixed Magic at all. In the summer of 2006 a very good friend of mine had his homie and cousin both shot in the same day, leaving one injured and the other dead. Another personal friend of mine was on the other end of the murder, and although he didn't pull the trigger he was there, and he did supply the firearm. I called Ricardo the next day to tell him that my mind was too cloudy to commit to a role at the moment. Eventually, he convinced me to come in as an assistant stage manager and massaged me into a role for *The Taming of the Shrew*, which was the best decision I ever made in my life. Now when I get faced with a crossroads of that kind, I already know what to do. *Moby-Dick*, Mixed Magic Theatre, Trish Botkin, NML did more than just teach me about an old book. They all played a part in saving my life.

Excerpt from the poem "Baggy Jeans"

Our community has half of our young kids doing life bids
Selling dope to dope fiends itching for a fix
Laying decaying six feet deep in a ditch
Slain in disagreements that turn into murders quick
So I turn poverty into poetry every time I spit
Using rhythmic rhetoric for a riotous influence of righteousness
On the corner hustling but knowledge is my product
This hustle you can't knock it, I cop it from my connect
Life and college, investing in love letting my soul get the prophet
Flipping an ounce of negativity to a kilo of positivity
Cooking up wisdom selling all my people prosperity
Life in this world is constantly full of casualties
I turn losses to motivation, optimism is my therapy
So next time you wonder why my jeans are so big
Understand every time I put them on I think of all this
Bigger Pants Bigger Pockets to fit more things

Like the mental notes I write to find happiness
In this world where love is close to extinct
My big pants are past just a fad to me
It has a deeper means
To keep a sky full of sunshine in the pocket of my baggy jeans

—Rudy "Rudacious" Cabrera

CHAPTER 6

Four Readers 3

Reading *Moby-Dick* as a Literary Scholar

Wyn Kelley

I have been reading *Moby-Dick* happily since the 1970s. In that time the book's cultural significance and meanings have changed tremendously, not just for me or for academics but for U.S. culture and the world. *Moby-Dick* is one of the United States' most inexhaustible and renewable resources.

When I first approached the book in college, it was at the height of its reputation as a Great American Classic. As later 20th-century critics have argued, Melville's novel rose to its 20th-century prominence in the wake of World War II as an assertion of U.S. cultural as well as political power. Ahab was read at midcentury as a tragic figure and the book as a meditation on flawed greatness. The postwar New Critics and in particular F. O. Matthiessen, who coined the phrase "the American Renaissance," enshrined Melville in a White, New England canon that included Hawthorne, Emerson, Thoreau, and Emily Dickinson. Their view of art as guided by certain rules demanded that a book have a unified form and intention (they particularly favored tragedy, a form that only barely made sense of the book's vastness and variety); that it take its place in a literary elite (thus the strong interest in echoes of Shakespeare, Milton, Greek drama, and the Bible); and that it also include certain modern aesthetic principles, such as irony, use of complex symbolism, formal unity and coherence, and "deep" meaning embedded in the story. Reading the book in this context meant combing its images for patterns of meaning, searching out sources that indicated its literary allusiveness and richness, and pondering its themes and philosophy.

How were we to know that Melville's 19th-century readers would have rejected this form of reading outright, responding instead to the adventure narrative and balking at what they saw as metaphysical "blubber"? Yet the work of writing about Melville's life and reputation proceeded for most of the first half of the 20th century under the assumption that Melville was a misunderstood genius—not a briefly popular writer of nautical adventures. If his contemporaries did not see that genius, 20th-century conventional wisdom decreed, then they were common benighted folk, unable to appreciate a tragic hero in their midst, unlike the academic critics of a later time. But this view didn't necessarily pertain outside academia. I remember having dinner with friends in Stockholm in the 1980s. A female Swedish journalist leaned over and said, "But why are you writing your dissertation on Herman Melville? Didn't he write boys' books?" To this sophisticated European, most of 19th-century American fiction, from Cooper's *The Last of the Mohicans* to Twain's *The Adventures of Huckleberry Finn*, was children's literature—hardly the stuff of neglected genius.

By the time I entered graduate school in the late 1970s, critics had begun to reject the New Critical notion of the text as inviolable work of art and to place it in a broader historical and cultural context. Trained as a New Historicist, I wrote my thesis on Melville's New York and the urban culture that he responded to as strongly as he did to the sea. My work and that of many others attempted to knock Melville off the American Renaissance pedestal by placing him in company with a wider range of authors—in my case, popular sensational urban writers like George Lippard and George C. Foster, as well as the producers of new urban forms like the panorama, the sketch, and the urban travel narrative. But another wave of criticism was emerging at the same time, the one to which my Swedish interlocutor also implicitly referred: feminism. Why was I, a woman, writing about a dead White male author? At that point I had proceeded too far with my dissertation to change course. But as someone who entered graduate school as a single working woman and left as a wife and mother of two small children, I naturally thought long and hard about the implications of studying Melville when the canon was now exploding with new authors like Harriet Beecher Stowe, Lydia Maria Child, Fanny Fern, and Harriet Jacobs.

Yet curiously enough, over the next couple of decades *Moby-Dick* went from being understood as a book about tragic greatness, with Ahab as hero, to being interpreted as a reflection of democratic inclusiveness, with Ishmael as its wise, comic voice. The 1990s saw an outpouring of new readings of the book's multicultural themes and multiracial characters: Queequeg, Daggoo, Tashtego, and Pip. Feminists found their way to the novel, as more women joined the ranks of Melville scholars, challenging the notion that Melville spoke only for men in a patriarchal culture. As explorations of gender in *Moby-Dick* became more subtle, the book also attracted readings of its sexual themes, in particular the homoerotic (and interracial) friendships between Ishmael and Queequeg, or Ahab and Pip.

In the same period (and also more recently), while all these approaches continued to inspire new readers, critical interest also shifted to Melville's other works and their social themes, creative innovations, and developing concerns. Study of stories like "Bartleby, the Scrivener," "Benito Cereno," "The Paradise of Bachelors and the Paradise of Maids," or "Billy Budd"; of novels like *Typee, Pierre*, and *The Confidence-Man*; or of Melville's large and neglected body of poetry has somewhat displaced *Moby-Dick* as the previously unchallenged "masterpiece" and opened up new ways of thinking about it. This direction in academic studies runs somewhat counter, though, to the abiding centrality of *Moby-Dick* in popular culture, and over time that phenomenon has been studied too by cultural historians and, more recently, media scholars. The recognition that *Moby-Dick* exists in multiple media and social forms—film, television, comic books, fine arts and illustration, music, and restaurants—and has continued to exert a pull over new readers and consumers of the text makes its reach and importance even greater than before.

Melville, of course, would be tickled at the attention and perhaps mystified by it at the same time. For a literary scholar, as this necessarily broad sweep through the recent critical history must indicate, reading *Moby-Dick* has meant continually changing lenses as the book undergoes new interpretations. In this latest iteration, the New Media Literacies approach, the book has made me rethink my own practices as reader.

MOBY-DICK AND LITERACY

As much as I've changed my critical positions and practices over many years, I still cling to traditional habits of reading. The product of a mother who spent hours reading to her children and a father who taught high school English and revered Melville (and Chaucer, Faulkner, Shakespeare, and Eliot) in precisely the mid-20th-century ways I've described above, I've inherited both the wholehearted love of books—that desire to be swept away that I think of as Romantic—and the longing to probe and understand that I call Critical.

We might also associate these modes of reading with a right-brain immersion in sensuous and imaginative experience as opposed to a left-brain navigation of the text, complete with charts, guides, and lists. Or we might distinguish between the way Ishmael reads—fluidly, enthusiastically, according to his boundless curiosity and inventive thinking—and the way Ahab approaches reading, using maps and whaling chronicles with a definite plan or goal. One form of reading replicates the Sublime, in that we are drawn irresistibly into the text, seduced, horrified, or intoxicated by something greater than ourselves; the other gives us an experience of the Beautiful, in all its symmetry and harmony, its order that calms and elevates the mind. One might be called Dionysian, the other Apollonian. One is House, the other Senate. And so on.

Students, in my experience, approach reading with both approaches in mind. They love the experience of losing themselves in a text, and they also savor the joy of discovering themselves and mastering their world. We do them a disservice if we try to separate those two modes of reading or prioritize them, suggesting that one exists only for private pleasure, the other for public instruction and assessment. One is for enjoyment, we seem to be telling them, the other learning. One is emotional, the other rational. One has no particular meaning; anything you think is fine. The other has a meaning assigned by teachers, critics, and other authorities; whatever you think, you must eventually adopt this authoritative interpretation. But we have a bicameral government and a bicameral brain. We arrive at understanding through complex negotiations between different parts of ourselves. Melville understood this when he gave his book both a narrator, Ishmael, and a protagonist, Ahab; a Sperm Whale balanced by a Right Whale; and endless pairings of light and dark, calm and storm, masthead reverie and forecastle revelry, human passion and nature's indifference and inscrutability. Although he also delights in playing off his pairs against threes (Queequeg, Daggoo, and Tashtego, or Starbuck, Stubb, and Flask) and then endless multiples—of whales, of authors—he keeps coming back to his basic dyads and the stabilizing balance between them.

Moby-Dick teaches us, then, to value two (at least) modes of reading. Teachers can open up the experience of reading to include all its dimensions and possibilities, build on students' strengths, and negotiate both sides of their minds and of literacy. Doing so would offer a creative personalized approach to texts, as well as a critical one.

In this endless balancing act, students would learn that, as Ishmael points out in Chapter 11, "Nightgown," "there is no quality in this world that is not what it is merely by contrast. Nothing exists in itself." Ishmael is describing the sensation of being in bed: To feel utterly warm some part of you must be very cold. When you have that double sensation, you can fully appreciate your situation: "Then there you lie like one warm spark in the heart of an arctic crystal." The startling juxtaposition of "spark" and "crystal," "warm" and "arctic," lying in bed and resting at the heart of a glacier, speaks to the novel's constant pattern of opposing unlike "duplicates." These juxtapositions light sparks, cause certain shocks to occur. We know that reading can produce these shocks, especially when *all* parts of the mind are engaged.

HOW DO LITERARY SCHOLARS THINK?

I expect that each of us representing four perspectives on reading—the creative producer, performer, media scholar, and literary scholar—might consider his or her approach the default position for all readers. After all, each of us was a "general" reader before becoming "specialized," and each would also reject an exclusive position that isolated others. Nothing I do, in other words, seems to me that different from what other readers do, too. At the same time, we also contribute different methods, different kinds of awareness. For me, one critical emphasis in literary study is its concern with artful uses of language.

We use artful language all the time, in both daily speech and different media. As Ricardo Pitts-Wiley reminds us, artful language appears in Shakespeare's plays and on street corners; he argues that if Shakespeare were alive today, he would be listening to and borrowing from the latest slang expressions, hip-hop coinages, slogans, and rants. There is nothing special about finding artful language in Melville when you can find it likewise in a blog or an ad or a movie. The question is, How do we know it's artful? And how does recognizing its artfulness expand our awareness of human beings, ourselves, and our world?

Toni Morrison (1992) addresses this problem when she writes, in *Playing in the Dark*, about her discovery that classic American White-authored fiction always contains an implicit "Africanist" presence, a fugitive, generally invisible Other whose special status makes possible the author's assumptions of his or her own freedom, democracy, and liberality—the founding principles, supposedly, of American government and the American dream. She describes the impact of this discovery as being like the experience of watching a goldfish and suddenly becoming aware of the bowl: "It's as if I had been looking at a fishbowl—the glide and flick of the golden scales, the green tip, the bolt of white careening back from the gills; the castles at the bottom, surrounded by pebbles, the flecks of waste and food, the tranquil bubbles traveling to the surface—and suddenly I saw the bowl, the structure that transparently (and invisibly) permits the ordered life it contains to exist in the larger world" (p. 17). We think we swim in a transparent medium, that all our thoughts and decisions come freely from ourselves. We fail to see the hard invisible substance that shapes and contains our movements.

Likewise, we all live in a world of language without, often, seeing the bowl—the interests that form and shape that language, that give value to certain kinds or uses of language over others, that judge and decide for us as much as we do for ourselves. This metaphor may seem a depressing reminder of how little we understand and control our environments. But it can also, as Morrison shows, free and empower us, and teach us to understand and maybe leap out of the bowl, imaginatively, at least. Knowing how language works, how it shapes us and how we can shape it, gives power. Literacy, as countless writers tell us, confers more than social status. It can change the meaning of our lives. But literacy, as Morrison suggests, involves more than reading text. It includes understanding how language works.

And artfulness? *Artful* has both positive and negative connotations. In its association with creativity and imagination, skill and taste, it suggests the highest forms of human invention and aspiration. In its other meanings of "manipulative," "clever," "subtle," and "sneaky," it reminds us that we had better watch out. In relation to what we teach our students in the classroom, artfulness also has double and potentially conflicting meanings. We want to prepare our students for the "real" world, not, in most cases, for the world of art. Yet artful people in the real world may create obstacles for artless youth, and so we need to prepare them.

The one tool that I see as essential for the literary critic, the student, the professional, or the amateur, the one traditional but perennially useful skill in literary study and in all kinds of media texts is close reading. We have different words for this practice. Some of my students dismissively call it "dissecting" the text, with the clear understanding that a text must be dead to be dissected. *Analyzing* it has a similar connotation, except that since we analyze data of all kinds and in other fields, at least we might be conducting something similar to a scientific experiment or mathematical proof. But it is certainly not creative. *Digging in* implies that the surface is uninteresting and that only the depths, after much labor, will yield up the improbable ore we seek. But it's so much work! *Unpacking* conveys a more accessible approach; but what are we looking for when we unpack? And how do we know we've found something valuable?

To me, close reading, like other forms of closeness, implies intimacy and familiarity. Just as you do not ask certain probing or embarrassing questions on a first date, you do not expect to know more than the facts on a first reading. In a literary text, that means somewhat adequately understanding the plot, the characters, and their motives and recognizing certain patterns, images, or repetitions of thematic consequence. We can teach and test this knowledge fairly reliably, since it communicates to most readers. It is not superficial knowledge, but we can know it without reading closely, without in fact consciously taking account of the language, the medium, in which we received it.

So, on a first date, you pay attention to *what* your new acquaintance has to say, as you mentally sift these facts and decide if you want to go on a second date. By the tenth encounter, perhaps, you have become more aware of *why* this person says these things and *how*, what they *mean* in a context that includes your closer observation of how he or she dresses, chews gum, laughs, talks to parents or friends, makes or does not make the bed, chooses music, or drives a car. Furthermore you begin to recognize how this person makes you feel, and that reaction tells you something not only about him or her but also about yourself, since in every relationship we act in old and new ways. Similarly, closer reading of a text allows us to experience and learn more in a dynamic relationship between what the author has put on the page and what we actually take in. The text begins to have meaning for us in more varied and subtle ways, and we begin to feel that we know it better. So we judge and have opinions. Just as we begin to argue with the person we know better than before, we begin to argue with a text or with the assumptions people have had about a text. One can measure that kind of knowledge best, perhaps, through writing assignments that allow students to develop critical opinions, explore the complexity of their responses, and communicate their differences with other readers.

Again, however, you may swim in this kind of understanding without taking much account of the fact that you are in a certain kind of water— language shaped by a certain kind of bowl, the meaning we attach to certain uses of language. Perhaps the best way to think of this problem is to imagine understanding your new love after he or she has left. As you sort through the old emails and photos wondering why this person dumped you (or you dumped him or her), as you reevaluate the messages you received before, picking up the dirty socks and seeing them in the clear light of your new and shocked understanding that this person you loved is not who you thought he or she was at all, you are now reading closely in a new way. You are reading the person not in the flesh but through the media in which you know that person now—through photos, discarded belongings, and old notes. And instead of focusing on the person, you begin to sift the *language* of this person. What does that language tell you now that the person has gone? And what does that language tell you about the way humans communicate with each other and conduct their relationships? You can ask the same questions about the reports you wrote for a job after you've left it or about the diaries you wrote ages ago. We read these texts closely, not only as they appear to us at first but also as they have meaning later. As we do, we necessarily detach ourselves from the person and pay more attention to the medium. What does an old sock say? How does a diary communicate? What do these different kinds and uses of language tell us about our ways of creating meaning?

Harriet Beecher Stowe reflects on this phenomenon in her novel *The Minister's Wooing* (1859/1999) when she addresses the reader directly about the power of the things people leave behind: "Have not ribbons, cast-off flowers, soiled bits of gauze, trivial, trashy fragments of millinery sometimes had an awful meaning, a deadly power, when they belonged to one who should wear them no more? . . . You are living your daily life among trifles that one death-stroke may make relics" (pp. 120–121). She is talking about how a casual object associated with a living person becomes a relic, a treasure, after that person dies. Such objects revive memory and inspire close reading and rereading, because we long to understand what is now irreparably past. And what once seemed real, but unremarkable, like the goldfish bowl, can often come to seem artful, as these objects acquire histories and we see in them more complex forces at work than the actions of everyday life.

Similarly texts of all kinds, if we know and love them well, come to seem in time precious and worth examining more closely. When we teach close reading we are engaging a number of other life skills: the ability to reflect meaningfully on what we know and how we know it, the recognition that we use language in subtle ways and that we can learn more about them, the awareness that meanings change over time and circumstance and that reading and rereading teach us how to appreciate and make sense of those shifts and shocks.

CHAPTER 7

Four Readers 4

Reading (*Moby-Dick*) as a Media Scholar

Henry Jenkins

A cartoon captures some of the contradictions surrounding the relations between my field, media studies, and the ways that literature is most often taught in American high schools: A glowering teacher confronts a student, who is holding a paper that displays his poor grade on an assignment, and the caption says, "The tip off was your reference to Gregory Peck's obsession with the Great White Whale."

I could have been that student standing there. When I was assigned *Moby-Dick* in my high school English class, I never got past the chapter "The Whiteness of the Whale." By that point, I had read a children's illustrated edition, had devoured the Classics Illustrated comics version, and had seen the Gregory Peck film several times. I *loved Moby-Dick*, though my teacher, Mrs. Hopkins, did little to capitalize on my existing familiarity with the story through other media. Like the teacher in the cartoon, she viewed those other media versions with suspicion; consuming them was cheating, trying to get away without reading the book, and little else. Needless to say, we didn't see eye to eye.

Somehow, reading *Moby-Dick* was very different from simply experiencing the story. Melville kept interrupting the adventure story elements that I knew from the other versions with ponderous meditations, encyclopedic discussions of whales and whaling, sermons, bits of theatrical scripts, and detailed character descriptions. I had no clue what to do with this other material, and my teacher didn't provide much help. We were assigned the task of writing a paper on biblical allusions in the novel, but I hadn't really been taught what allusions were or what one might say about them. I never finished reading the novel. I wrote what was probably the worst essay I ever wrote in high school; I got a bad grade on it, and I decided I never wanted to read that stupid book again!

All that changed when I met Ricardo Pitts-Wiley and listened to him talk about his plans to stage a contemporary version of *Moby-Dick*. For one thing, Ricardo is a hard guy to say no to. He speaks with a deep booming voice, which carries an enormous amount of passion and conviction. For another, his vision of getting young people to read and rewrite *Moby-Dick* was very much in line with my own strongly held belief that in order to reach the current generation, for whom mashup videos and resampled music have become defining aesthetic experiences, we need to help them learn through remixing. So many MIT students through the years have told me that they learned about technology by taking things apart, tinkering with them, putting them back together, and trying to figure out what makes them work. And I've found myself wondering how we can carry some of those same experiences into the humanities classroom.

As a media scholar, I've been studying for more than 25 years how readers read and what fans do with their favorite programs. For much of that time, I have been researching the phenomenon of fan fiction. Fans dig deep into their favorite television programs, films, and novels; draw out interesting elements; and elaborate upon them through original stories and novels. I had watched a growing number of people getting into the fan writing world by the time they reached middle or high school. I've spoken with 14- and 15-year-olds who have, for example, written full-length *Harry Potter* novels, which they post to the web and which get hundreds of comments from readers around the world (Jenkins, 2006a).

I've argued that writing fan fiction represents a particularly valuable form of criticism, one that breaks all the rules I was taught in school—getting inside the heads of the characters rather than trying to decipher what the author meant, speculating beyond the ending rather than taking the text as given, asserting one's own fantasies and interests rather than working to recover hidden meanings (Jenkins, 1992). Yet it also led to new insights and discoveries, as young writers performed close readings and debated interpretations, mobilizing passages from the text in the process. Fan fiction is a form of criticism that sees the original work as the starting point for a conversation, one that, as Mrs. Hopkins might have put it, sees the original story as a "living" element in our contemporary culture.

If young writers could do this with *Harry Potter* or *Naruto*, *Lord of the Rings* or *X-Men*, then why can't they do it with Melville, Hawthorne,

Shakespeare, or Austen? And that's precisely what Pitts-Wiley is doing, working with students who are not only "at risk" but already incarcerated, the kids that most people have already given up on. If he could get those young convicts to read *Moby-Dick*, then what excuse do I have as an adult academic for not reading it?

So I dug out the same battered old Bantam paperback edition that defeated me in high school, and I read through it, chapter by chapter, the yellowed pages peeling off the spine in my hands. I discovered a very different book from the one I remembered. *Moby-Dick* made much more sense when understood not as a classically constructed work but rather as a mashup. Melville absorbed as much of 19th-century whaling lore as he could, mixing it with elements borrowed from the Bible, Milton, Homer, Shakespeare, and countless other writers; he produced something that shifted between genres, adopted a range of different voices and perspectives, and refused to deliver what we anticipate from one page to the next. The very parts that frustrated me as a high school student fascinated me as an adult.

Some of this has to do with the particular qualities of *Moby-Dick* as a novel and Herman Melville as a writer. Yet don't stop there. The Russian literary critic Mikhail Bakhtin (1981) tells us that writers don't take their words from the dictionary but extract them from other people's mouths and these words come to us still dripping with saliva. As my mother used to say, "Put that down. You don't know where it's been." But in this case, we do know where it's been. It has a history. It's already part of our culture. Writers don't create in a vacuum. For all our celebration of originality, authors draw heavily on stories, images, ideas that are circulating all around them. They take inspiration from other books, just as fan fiction writers take inspiration from J. K. Rowling.

Indeed, that's what Mrs. Hopkins was trying to get us to understand when she asked us to write about biblical allusions in *Moby-Dick*. She wanted us to see how Melville was retelling stories from the Bible, giving them new meanings, and inserting them into new contexts. Melville was a great writer and a gifted storyteller, but it didn't mean he made everything up out of his head. Melville and the other writers we study in high school literature classes borrowed from everything they had ever read, yet in the process of remixing those elements, retooling that language, and retelling those stories, they created something that felt fresh and original to their readers. Bakhtin (1981) tells us that writers have to battle with their materials, forcing them to mean what they want them to mean, trying to shed some associations and accent others. The borrowed material is never fully theirs; it leaves traces of its previous use, traces we can follow like so many bread crumbs back to their sources, and in the process we can see Melville and these other authors speak to and about what came before.

MEDIA (AND LITERACY) IN TRANSITION

We are living through a moment of media change during which more and more average people are becoming authors. And young people—the students in your class, sometimes even the ones who are sitting at the back of your class and not saying anything—are at the cutting edge of this shift toward a more participatory culture. A study conducted by the Pew Center for the Internet and American Life (Lenhart & Madden, 2005) found that 60% of American teens online have produced media and about a third of them have shared media they've produced with others beyond their immediate friends and family, and about a quarter of them have created new content by remixing existing content.

The Pew Center statistic is interesting on two levels: First, it tells us that there are a lot of young authors trying to make sense of their own creative processes, and second, it tells us that there are large numbers of teens who are being left behind what I call the *participation gap*. While some people in your classes have had the thrill of seeing people they didn't even know read and respond to something they created, others have no such experience and may not feel empowered to create or share what they create with others.

Neither of these groups is well served when we mystify the act of authorship in our literature classes. Beginning writers need to draw on models and take inspiration from other stories they have read, but the dirty little secret is that so do gifted writers. They are taking materials from their culture and deploying them as raw materials to manufacture something new. Thinking about authorship in those terms, as a cultural process, allows us to revitalize some of the things literature scholars have always done—talking about sources, exploring allusions, comparing different works within the same genre, watching an author's vision take shape over multiple works. All these approaches help us to see that writers are also readers and that understanding their acts of reading can help us to better understand their writing.

If we can follow this process backward in time, tracing how Melville read and reworked material from the Bible to create *Moby-Dick*, we can also trace it forward in time, looking at how other creators, working in a range of different media, took elements from *Moby-Dick* and used them as inspiration for their own creative acts. That's what Ricardo Pitts-Wiley did when he wrote and staged *Moby-Dick: Then and Now*. It's also what the incarcerated youth did when they participated in his workshop and learned how to read and rewrite *Moby-Dick*. Talking with Pitts-Wiley, I saw that he didn't view remixing as a matter of turning kids loose with the text to do what they want with it; he insisted that remixing must begin with a close reading and deep understanding of the original work.

MEDIATING MELVILLE

And that brings us back to the teacher, the student, and poor maligned Gregory Peck. The teacher in the cartoon sees the act of watching the film as a form of cheating because the student didn't read the novel, but there are other ways to look at the problem. Filmmakers started adapting *Moby-Dick* for the screen as early as 1926. The novel was already known and loved by their culture; filmmakers wanted to borrow literary prestige for a then emerging medium through adopting books with middle-class respectability (Uricchio & Pearson, 1993). Each filmmaker selected which elements to take from the novel. In the process, each created an individual emphasis and developed a singular interpretation, rethinking and reworking the novel according to the particulars of the medium (rejecting passages that would be boring to play out in real time or prohibitively expensive to film) and reflecting the tastes and interests of that filmmaker's own time.

Each of the films—including the 1956 Gregory Peck movie—represents a distinctive interpretation of Melville's novel, and each helps us to discover new things about *Moby-Dick*. All these versions should be understood as expansions on rather than replacements for the experience of reading the original novel. And a good teacher can draw on bits and pieces of these adaptations to help spark debates in his or her classes about interpretation, appropriation, and creativity. It is not that adaptations offer us a pre-digested version of the novel; each of these works poses its own kind of challenges for the viewer/reader. We tend to devalue the skills involved in reading a film because they often were not acquired through formal education; we learned them through informal everyday practices such as watching a movie with our parents and asking them a painfully large number of questions about what was going on. Mrs. Hopkins and others with her outlook devalue screen experiences because they say that these don't demand as much of the imagination as reading does. In fact, there are trade-offs: Screen adaptations do take away some of the imaginative work of novel reading because they can show us what things look like, yet they may demand more work on other levels, such as figuring out the inner life of the characters through externalized gestures.

One of the things media scholars do is to trace what we call migratory stories, stories that get told over and over again as they move across different media and across national borders. We want to understand what changes as the same story gets told in different contexts by different authors for different audiences through different media. And we find this activity works best when we compare multiple versions that share similar themes and inspiration.

As a media scholar, I have been taught to suspend judgment about the line separating high and popular culture. We know that this border has shifted dramatically over time. Many works taught in literature classes (by Shakespeare, Dickens) were once regarded as popular culture. And many of the attacks currently directed against contemporary popular culture were also once directed against the novel or theater. Each medium has to be evaluated on its own terms—not as a debased form of literature but as an aesthetic tradition with its own standards of accomplishment. Some approaches to literature seek to narrow and refine students' tastes, weaning them from their attachments to popular culture. My own approach seeks to broaden students' tastes and expand the range of works with which they can meaningfully engage.

FROM READERS TO AUTHORS

And, for me, it doesn't end there—with teaching students to be gifted "readers" of texts across many different media, worthy though that goal may be. Rather, we want them to think of themselves as people who could become authors, people who are able to make creative and meaningful contributions to their culture, and people who have thought through the ethical dimensions of appropriation. And that's part of the value of having young people not simply read classic literature but also rewrite it, remake it, across a broad range of different media. In encouraging this, we help prepare them to join in a culture that is far more open to the participation of average citizens than ever before.

Going back to the Pew study, we need to do this for the 60% who already are making media, to help give them a vocabulary for thinking about their own creative process, and we need to do this for the 40% who are not yet making media, as we help them find their own creative voices. By helping them learn that all writers were once readers and that every reader has the potential to become a writer, we help them to move across that participation gap. After all, we would not consider people literate in a traditional sense if they could read and not write; we should not consider them to have media literacy if they are critical consumers but do not know how to produce and circulate media.

A central guiding principle behind New Media Literacies' work is the belief that media literacy cannot and should not be divorced from the rest of the school curriculum, that it should not be an add-on subject at the end of the school week if the students have been good. Rather, the new media literacies should represent a paradigm shift that affects how we teach all aspects of the school curriculum, just as media change has affected every aspect of our society. Our goal is to show how the new media literacies might impact the teaching of literature. In carrying out this goal, we hope that teachers can help heighten students' understanding of media and broaden their skills as readers and cultural participants; but we also hope that paying attention to how authors build on existing cultural materials and how later creators build on their work will make students better readers of literature and help foster the deep appreciation that a novel like *Moby-Dick* deserves.

CHAPTER 8

Motives for Reading

Fan Culture, Pop Culture, and Collaborative Reading Practices

Henry Jenkins

The study of how and why readers read has become an important sub-field of media and cultural studies. Work in this tradition ranges from the study of the personal associations formed by individual readers as they encounter canonical literary texts to research into large-scale "interpretive communities," such as the fandoms that emerge around popular television shows, films, comics, and literary genres. The way we teach students to read in schools represents one possible way of reading a text, an institutionally specific set of practices that emerge from the field of literary studies. This approach is valuable, to be sure, but may be radically different from what readers do with books when they choose to read them on their own. Indeed, students often experience a disconnect between the two sets of activities. For those students for whom reading in school is a struggle, their displeasure may block them from picking up books in their everyday life. In other words, we may be teaching them *not* to read even as we think we are teaching them *how* to read.

So, in this section, I want to call educators' attention to the range of motives and purposes that shape the reading of popular media texts; my hope is to give you some background on the range of different experiences and perspectives your students bring into the classroom. This focus will encourage you and your students to "go meta"—that is, to pay attention to how and why they are reading a difficult book like *Moby-Dick*. Rather than ignore those elements that make Melville's novel challenging, we want you to acknowledge those challenges and to help students broaden their strategies for confronting them. When I studied *Moby-Dick* in high school, my teacher, Mrs. Hopkins, had a very clear motive for why I was supposed to be reading the book—to find allusions to the Bible—which had little or nothing to do with my own reasons for wanting to read the book, which were that I had enjoyed the film version and wanted to spend more time in Melville's world.

These different motives, in turn, require different strategies for reading. Literary scholar Peter J. Rabinowitz (1985) argues that genre, for example, represents less a category of texts than an approach to reading. He suggests that genre involves "reading *as*." My teacher was encouraging me to read *Moby-Dick* as a retelling of the biblical story of Jonah, while I was reading *Moby-Dick as* the story of men against whales. Rabinowitz argues that the choice of a genre involves alternative strategies for interpretation. First, he talks about "rules of notice" that give priority to certain aspects of narratives as potentially significant while assigning others to the margins. No one can pay attention to every detail in a book as expansive as *Moby-Dick*, but how do we decide what to notice? Second, genre sets "rules of signification" that determine what meanings can be ascribed to the significant details we've identified. How do I know what the white whale means? Third, "rules of configuration" shape the reader's expectations about likely plot developments. We know that when Ahab and his crew find the whale, they are not likely to give him a big hug or fire machine guns or tap dance on his back or try to communicate his songs to visitors from another world. Fourth, "rules of coherence" shape the extrapolations readers make. Once we have read a book, certain questions linger. What, for example, happened to Ahab's son? Depending on our goals for reading, we may be encouraged to speculate further or forget about these loose ends.

Seeking insights into how people read literature, David Bleich (1986) asked male and female students to retell the plot of William Faulkner's "A Rose for Emily." He found significant differences in male and female responses. Male students read for authorial meaning, perceiving a "strong narrational voice" shaping events, while female students "experienced the narrative as a world" that exists beyond the short story. Male students tried to recover what Faulkner meant, while female students got inside the heads of the characters. The male students moved quickly to interpretation even when they were trying to recount the plot, while the female students felt freer to add their own speculations to their account. Not surprisingly, the males' reading strategy is the one most often promoted through the classroom, where the author's voice is seen as more important than the characters', and where recovering meanings is valued more than speculating about what might happen after the story ends. Yet in promoting this strategy, we may be discouraging other forms of reading and motives for reading that are also rewarding.

In one of my early research projects (Tulloch & Jenkins, 1995), I looked at three very different communities of readers who were invested in the television series *Star Trek*: mostly male MIT students; mostly female fan fiction writers; and the Galaxians, a group of gay, lesbian, and bisexual fans. The male MIT students were most interested in the technical aspects, classifying episodes based on which body of scientific knowledge they evoked, and using them as a starting point to speculate about future discoveries and innovations in their chosen disciplines. The female fans were much more interested in the strong emotional ties between the characters—romances, friendships, and community bonds. The Galaxians saw *Star Trek* as a social utopia that embraced diversity. These different motives affected what each group took away from the series. For example, when asked about each of the regular characters, the male MIT students described them as autonomous problem-solvers, identifying what actions they took to "save the ship," whereas the female fanzine writers read the characters through their relationships as mentors, friends, lovers, and shipmates. The male MIT students translated their enthusiasm for the series into "nitpicking," criticizing errors in the science, making models of ships, or playing computer and role-playing games centered on combat situations. The female fans responded by writing stories, especially stories that loosely fell into the romance genre, and making music videos, which likewise focused on the emotional lives of the characters.

WHAT DO WE READ FOR?

The web has made it much easier for us to see different groups of readers in the process of reading favorite texts. We can take those insights back with us into the classroom as we think about what might be going on inside the heads of different students, each with his or her own motives that shape what he or she is likely to get out of a book. We might start with the basic question—What are you reading for?—and realize that different readers pay attention to different kinds of information.

Sample Fan Websites

Cataloging and Collecting

The Patrick O'Brian Compendium: http://www.patrickobrian.com/

Nitpicking

The Continuity Errors Section of the *Battlestar Galactica* Wiki:
http://en.battlestarwiki.org/wiki/Continuity_errors_

Speculating

Theories on *Lost*: http://www.theoriesonlost.com/
Survivor: Why They Lost: http://www.realitynewsonline.com/cgi-bin/ae.pl?mode
=1&article=article7926.art&page=1

Recapping

Television Without Pity: http://www.televisionwithoutpity.com

Consider, for example, The Patrick O'Brian Compendium, a website where readers of a popular series of sea novels have pooled information, each tackling a different body of knowledge. On this site, you can see, for example, a breakdown of all the medical issues (wounds and diseases) the characters confronted and how they were cured; other readers have cataloged the ships or developed a time line of the events, researched vintage recipes or produced a glossary of old naval terms. Looking at this site, one can imagine readers going through the books with yellow highlighters, marking different passages. That's precisely what I hope will happen in your classrooms as you encourage students to identify their own interests in *Moby-Dick*.

As we turn toward other fan websites and discussion lists, we may also pay attention to the different things readers *do* with texts. For example, another website, now defunct, communicated a medical student's reactions to *House M.D.* For each episode, he identified the medical issues and practices depicted and critiqued them from his own professional knowledge and experience. Fans call this approach "nitpicking" (see Jenkins, 2007a). While one can have an entertaining episode, which misrepresents medical information, the medical student also takes pleasure in testing his own evolving knowledge against the series.

The Continuity Errors section of the *Battlestar Galactica* Wiki involves a different form of nitpicking: It is primarily focused on identifying continuity errors, places where the program contradicts earlier information. Fans collectively see if they can spot the mistakes and thus demonstrate their mastery over complex long-form narratives.

Lost is famous for its mysteries and puzzles (Jenkins, 2006b). Whether you like the series or not depends on your interest in these enigmas. Theories on *Lost* became a place where fans could share and evaluate their theories. Fans might describe this activity as speculation.

For many seasons, *Survivor* fan David Bloomberg explained why the contestant booted that week lost the game. Over time, he developed some core questions he asked about the contestants' strategies, identifying mistakes they made and, in the process, anticipating which characters will be voted off the island next. The events *Survivor* depicts have already occurred by the time the episodes reach the air: *Survivor* "spoilers" seek to determine what happened before they are told by the producers, a complex process which involves a mix of detective work and speculation (Jenkins, 2006a).

A site like Television Without Pity involves another fan practice: the recap. Here, amateur and professional writers summarize what happened for the benefit of those who missed an episode. The tone of this site is snarky—the writers enjoy the series, but part of their enjoyment stems from not taking the series too seriously.

Some of what readers do online looks very much like what readers do in classrooms: They form interpretations, often by tracing allusions to other works, as occurs in one fan's account of religious and mythological allusions in *The Matrix* franchise.

A striking feature of all these sites is that they represent a social process of reading. Fans go online to talk with other readers who are engaging with the same books and television shows. As they do so, sharing their reading experiences allows them to grow closer, forming friendships with others through their common reading practices. Here, readers may also debate different ways of interpreting shared texts and, in so doing, they often spell out their assumptions about the nature of reading. Fans engage in close readings, citing specific passages, debating interpretations, and constructing arguments to support their analysis. Fans often say that such conversations open a favorite series to new interpretations, allowing them to see things they might have missed and providing them new motives to watch the episodes again.

These fan discussion forums illustrate one of the core new media literacy skills—*collective intelligence*. These communities of readers operate in a world where nobody knows everything, everybody knows something, and what is known by any member is available to the group as a whole on demand. The NML white paper defines collective intelligence as "the ability to pool knowledge and compare notes with others towards a common goal" (Jenkins et al., 2009, p. xiv). Pierre Lévy (1997), who coined the term *collective intelligence*, states very clearly that a networked society is one where each participant develops a distinctive expertise that can contribute to the group's common ventures. People working together and sharing information are able to address questions far more complex and arrive at answers far more quickly than any single member could do. Such a social structure places great value on diversity: If each member contributes his or her own expertise, the community is strengthened by the diversity of its participants.

Right now, very few activities in schools support collective intelligence. Schools are still modeled on the ideal of the autonomous learner; individuals are expected to know everything within themselves and therefore seek nothing from others. To bring collective intelligence into the classroom, we first have to allow students to develop their own expertise and thus to take responsibility for helping the class to understand one aspect of the shared problem. Rather than having the students all read the same book for the same reasons, you can encourage the students to become more self-conscious about what they hope to get out of the book and allow them to pursue very different projects through their reading. In this way, they will not simply be trying to identify what their teacher thinks they should learn. Rather, they will be sharing with the teacher and their class what they discovered from reading the book in their own way.

HERMAN MELVILLE AS PROTO-FAN

A central premise of this book is that all authors were once readers, and their process of reading provides the preconditions for their acts of writing. In the discussion that follows, I will apply the vocabulary introduced above to what Melville does in writing about whaling culture. In other words, I want to read Melville as an enthusiast, perhaps even a fan, of whaling culture who wrote *Moby-Dick* to share his passion and interest with others.

Speculating

Here is one of the many passages in the book where Melville examines the story of Jonah:

> One old Sag-Harbor whaleman's chief reason for questioning the Hebrew story was this: He had one of those quaint old-fashioned Bibles, embellished with curious, unscientific plates; one of which represented Jonah's whale with two spouts in his head—a peculiarity only true with respect to a species of the Leviathan (the Right Whale, and the varieties of that order), concerning which the fishermen have this saying, "A penny roll would choke him"; his swallow is so very small. But, to this, Bishop Jebb's anticipative answer is ready. It is not necessary, hints the Bishop, that we consider Jonah as tombed in the whale's belly, but as temporarily lodged in some part of his mouth. And this seems reasonable enough in the good Bishop. For truly, the Right Whale's mouth would accommodate a couple of whist-tables, and comfortably seat all the players. Possibly, too, Jonah might have ensconced himself in a hollow tooth; but, on second thoughts, the Right Whale is toothless. —*Moby-Dick*, Chapter 83

In this case, he recounts a conversation among his fellow whaling fans—the old Sag-Harbor whaleman and Bishop Jebb—trying to make sense of contradictions in the source text. Their speculations extend beyond the information given in order to try to reconcile what they know of whales in the real world with what the story tells them about Jonah's encounter with the Leviathan. Contemporary fans would recognize the logic of this exchange: Melville takes an element that doesn't quite work in the original and, rather than discarding it, tries to figure out under what circumstances it might make sense. Fans often describe such creative work as "repairing the damage" created by a distracted artist who didn't think through all of the implications of his or her own story. What if we imagined Jonah inside the Whale's mouth rather than fully swallowed—maybe even inside his tooth? Ah, but these fans have already figured out that the Leviathan must have been a Right Whale, and not wanting to discard all that fan labor, they want to preserve that theory and so they have to discard this new layer of speculation.

Nitpicking

In this case, the speculations also constitute a form of nitpicking: The example above closely resembles the search for continuity errors on the *Battlestar Galactica* wiki. But we can also see evidence of the kind of interpretive practices demonstrated by the young doctor in training as he critiqued the representations of medical practice on *House M.D.* Such nitpicking comes through most vividly when Melville takes on previous representations of the whale. Here, we see Melville boldly assert his superior knowledge and his desire to "set the record straight," common motives for participation in fan discussion lists:

> I shall ere long paint to you as well as one can without canvas, something like the true form of the whale as he actually appears to the eye of the whaleman when in his own absolute body the whale is moored alongside the whaleship so that he can be fairly stepped upon there. It may be worth while, therefore, previously to advert to those curious imaginary portraits of him which even down to the present day confidently challenge the faith of the landsman. It is time to set the world right in this matter, by proving such pictures of the whale all wrong. —*Moby-Dick*, Chapter 55

But, before he can do so, he must clear away previous representations, in this case focusing on the anatomical inaccuracies created by artists who have had no direct experience of the living beast:

> These manifold mistakes in depicting the whale are not so very surprising after all. Consider! Most of the scientific drawings have been taken from the stranded fish; and these are about as correct as a drawing of a wrecked ship, with broken back, would correctly represent the noble animal itself in all its undashed pride of hull and spars. Though elephants have stood for their full-lengths, the living Leviathan has never yet fairly floated himself for his portrait. The living whale, in his full majesty and significance, is only to be seen at sea in unfathomable waters; and afloat the vast bulk of him is out of sight, like a launched line-of-battle ship; and out of that element it is a thing eternally impossible for mortal man to hoist him bodily into the air, so as to preserve all his mighty swells and undulations. And, not to speak of the highly presumable difference of contour between a young suckling whale and a full-grown Platonian Leviathan; yet, even in the case of one of those young sucking whales hoisted to a ship's deck, such is then the outlandish, eel-like, limbered, varying shape of him, that his precise expression the devil himself could not catch. —*Moby-Dick*, Chapter 55

I am reminded of a recurring feature on *Sequential Tarts*, a long-standing webzine by and for female comics fans, which regularly posts and critiques unlikely depictions of the female body in various superhero comics. Here, for example, is an excerpt from one tutorial on "Bizarre Breasts" (Malnassy, 2002):

> Bizarre proportions are nothing new to comics; be it the desire to cater to the cheesecake crowd or simply the preference of the artist, distorted anatomy has become commonplace. The fact that "professional" artists may utilize distortions in published works is a bit disappointing, but frankly, if they've gotten the job the odds are they aren't going to feel the need to change their style. That's fine, the world needs laughter. However, what does bother me is the possibility—hell, the reality—that amateur artists are copying this exaggerated anatomy and making these mistakes their own. So, in hopes of reaching those for whom this advice may actually have some impact, I have utilized my meager knowledge of anatomy and admittedly unpolished art skills to bring the world a brief tutorial on one of the comic artists' greatest challenges: the breast.

I don't want to push the parallels here too far, but both passages argue against the absurd and inaccurate representation of anatomy that comes from artists who don't really understand (and may have had limited exposure to) the subjects they are trying to depict.

Cataloging and Collecting

Melville, like modern-day fans, refuses to restrict himself to a single text or even a single mode of representation. As he explains, "There are some enterprises in which a careful disorderliness is the true method" (*Moby-Dick*, Chapter 82). And indeed, some of the most productive modes of fan interpretation involve rampant interdisciplinarity and free association, creating unexpected juxtapositions of texts, tracing real and imagined allusions to other works, as we saw in *The Matrix* example above. Melville read everything he could get his hands on—ancient books, religious texts, paintings, scrimshaw, currency, tavern signs, even the stars in the sky. He exhibits here the fan's fascination with cataloging and collecting:

> The more I dive into this matter of whaling, and push my researches up to the very spring-head of it so much the more am I impressed with its great honorableness and antiquity; and especially when I find so many great demi-gods and heroes, prophets of all sorts, who one way or other have shed distinction upon it, I am transported with

the reflection that I myself belong, though but subordinately, to so emblazoned a fraternity. —*Moby-Dick*, Chapter 82

I particularly like that last bit about becoming part of a "fraternity" of others who share his passions and knowledge, for this phrase conveys the social bonds within fan communities.

Appropriation and Transformation

Melville also appropriates and transforms the raw material, retelling classic stories for his own purposes. Consider how he roughly handles the canon in his retelling of the story of Saint George and the Dragon:

Akin to the adventure of Perseus and Andromeda—indeed, by some supposed to be indirectly derived from it—is that famous story of St. George and the Dragon; which dragon I maintain to have been a whale; for in many old chronicles whales and dragons are strangely jumbled together, and often stand for each other. "Thou art as a lion of the waters, and as a dragon of the sea," said Ezekiel; hereby, plainly meaning a whale; in truth, some versions of the Bible use that word itself. Besides, it would much subtract from the glory of the exploit had St. George but encountered a crawling reptile of the land, instead of doing battle with the great monster of the deep. Any man may kill a snake, but only a Perseus, a St. George, a Coffin, have the heart in them to march boldly up to a whale.

Let not the modern paintings of this scene mislead us; for though the creature encountered by that valiant whaleman of old is vaguely represented of a griffin-like shape, and though the battle is depicted on land and the saint on horseback, yet considering the great ignorance of those times, when the true form of the whale was unknown to artists; and considering that as in Perseus' case, St. George's whale might have crawled up out of the sea on the beach; and considering that the animal ridden by St. George might have been only a large seal, or sea-horse; bearing all this in mind, it will not appear altogether incompatible with the sacred legend and the ancientest draughts of the scene, to hold this so-called dragon no other than the great Leviathan himself. In fact, placed before the strict and piercing truth, this whole story will fare like that fish, flesh, and fowl idol of the Philistines, Dagon by name; who being planted before the ark of Israel, his horse's head and both the palms of his hands fell off from him, and only the stump or fishy part of him remained. Thus, then, one of our own noble stamp, even a whaleman, is the tutelary guardian of England; and by good rights, we harpooneers of Nantucket should be enrolled in the most noble order of St. George. And therefore, let not the knights of that honorable company (none of whom, I venture to say, have ever had to do with a whale like their great patron), let them never eye a Nantucketer with disdain, since even in our woollen frocks and tarred trowsers we are much better entitled to St. George's decoration than they. —*Moby-Dick*, Chapter 82

Fans might describe what Melville does here with Saint George as a What if? story: *What if* Saint George had been a seafaring rather than land-loving man? Indeed, we can see Melville as struggling with another fan community over which one of them "correctly" captures what is interesting about this character and his adventures.

But, like many later fans, Melville also struggles with how much fidelity the writer owes to the original source material. The author discusses the ways that multiple whalers approaching the same creature determine who can assert ownership over it, declaring some whales to be "fast-fish," that is, already harpooned and bound by a particular ship, and others to be "loose-fish," that is, free of any binds or constraints and thus subject to being grabbed by whichever ship approaches them first. Melville, then, extends this metaphor to talk about the work of the imagination: "What are you, reader, but a Loose-Fish and a Fast-Fish, too?" (*Moby-Dick,* Chapter 89). In other words, Melville is exploring to what degree we get hooked into a story and thus get captured by its author and to what degree our imagination remains unmoored, capable of taking the story wherever we want it to go. In a sense, that's exactly what fans are trying to make sense of when they debate how much they need to follow canon and to what degree they can construct their own fan universe. Read in this way, we can see *Moby-Dick*, often described as the Great American Novel, as a piece of fan fiction that grows out of Melville's fascination for the whale and his mastery over whaling lore. Drawing on a range of stories, responding to competing representations, Melville constructs his own original fiction, which he asserts better captures what fascinates him about man's eternal struggle against the natural order than previous representations.

CHAPTER 9

Finding Your Way and Leaving the Path

Wyn Kelley

This chapter gives readers tools for engaging with a new text and allows students to figure out why we are reading it. What are our *motives* for reading? How do we navigate this new place? Are there helpful signs? Can we recognize the author's very different motives in writing the story? Finally, we ask what happens if we go in an unanticipated direction or get off the path. The chapter shows how *Moby-Dick* addresses these questions.

In looking at motives, signs, and paths, we read in a way that is more like learning the terrain than getting to a destination. This book encourages readers to recognize and embrace nonlinear and discontinuous reading. With the skills and activities described in the rest of the chapter, students can raise their awareness of themselves as readers, enjoy the messiness of texts, and experience fewer inhibitions about navigating a challenging work like *Moby-Dick*.

MOBY-DICK AND NONLINEAR READING: WANDERING IN NEW TERRAIN

In *Moby-Dick*, Melville says: "There are some enterprises in which a careful disorderliness is the true method" (*Moby-Dick,* Chapter 82). His novel rewards "disorderliness" of reading because it is itself disorderly, though carefully so. Although it has a linear plot, structured around the quest for a whale, it deviates endlessly from its path. The last sentence of the book describes a ship wandering over the sea in a seemingly aimless pattern:

"It was the devious-cruising Rachel, that in her retracing search after her missing children, only found another orphan" (Epilogue). Melville uses the word *devious* not to mean "duplicitous" or "dishonest" but in its older sense of "circuitous" or "wandering." The reader of *Moby-Dick* is similarly "devious-cruising," invited to follow any number of paths through the narrative.

This disorderliness is precisely what makes many readers consider *Moby-Dick* a confusing and difficult book. It is long. It has digressions. Are we allowed to skim? How do we get through it?

We need not be scared off, though, by a book that seems disorderly. Melville and his readers *liked* long, digressive texts. The most popular writers of the era—Irving, Dickens, Hawthorne, Stowe, Twain, and Alcott, not to mention older favorites such as Cervantes, Rabelais, and Sterne—wrote books that by our standards are long and digressive, taking delight in lengthy description, numerous subplots, moral and philosophical musings, and considerable circuitousness in plotting. Melville's first and most popular book, *Typee*, fits this description perfectly. *Moby-Dick* was unpopular in its time, not because of its digressiveness—in that sense it was not particularly exceptional—but because it challenged certain social and racial taboos.

Indeed long, digressive books have appealed to enthusiastic readers throughout history. And older habits of reading—that is, reading nonlinearly, digressively, discontinuously, and selectively—have great value to us now as we navigate a wealth of new media. We propose reading *Moby-Dick* as Melville's readers might have read it—and as we read many forms of new media today.

To appreciate nonlinear reading, we need to identify linear reading. Reading literature, at least as understood for the past 150 years or so, has traditionally involved certain expectations of a text:

- It is linear. You start at the beginning and go to the end. Books have a design that you can best appreciate by reading in a given order.
- It is continuous. Books have a unity and cumulative effect that you would lose by jumping around.
- It is complete. You must read it all to get the meaning.
- It is deep. Your first reading gives you "only" surface understanding. You must read and reread, looking for significant patterns of language and theme, before you can say you understand the text.

This model applies to many kinds of texts, but especially to the classic literary fiction that many teachers use to train students in reading and language arts. Before the rise of the novel, however, in the early part of the 18th century, such a model of reading might not have appeared the norm for European and American readers. Before the mid-18th century, many Western readers, if they read at all, sampled from a wide variety of texts for which a linear reading would not have been necessary or even advisable: periodicals, almanacs, collections (of sermons, poetry, political speeches, essays, letters, tales, travel narratives, biographies), or encyclopedias. A work of history, biography, or philosophy might have required linear reading, but readers could explore a large field of books that did not.

A primary text for European and American culture, and a major influence on *Moby-Dick*, was the Bible. According to historians of the book, early modern readers and printers approached this long, often disorderly text with a number of "finding aids"—concordances, commentaries and annotations, illustrations, and maps—that made it possible to navigate the work in different ways, according to one's own interests (Stallybrass, 2002). Ministers selected and elaborated on particular passages for their sermons, rather than proceeding linearly through the text. Parishioners sometimes noted, collected, and annotated passages in what were called "commonplace books." In the periods before cut-and-paste digital technology, people created literary collections of their own by gathering favorite materials from other sources: moral tracts, poetry, sermons, fiction, and periodical essays. For those without formal education—especially women and members of the laboring classes—such personal collections compensated for the lack of books and instruction and allowed readers to pursue their own learning. As Matthew Brown (2007) argues, in "Undisciplined Reading," such habits emphasized "disorderly reading," a search for what concerns the reader rather than for mastery of the whole text.

The books that inspired Melville's writing of *Moby-Dick* include many that one would never read continuously from start to finish. Besides the Bible, Melville also loved travel books and encyclopedias, which in his day presented a cornucopia of information, lavishly illustrated and displayed. One of his favorite sources, the *Penny Cyclopaedia* (Long, 1833–1843), included topics from history, natural history, myth, popular culture, and science. Melville also read natural histories of whaling, such as Thomas Beale's *The Natural History of the Sperm Whale* (1839), where one might browse through information on whales, whaling paraphernalia, oceanography, anatomy, personal anecdotes from sailors and captains, and the history of "the fishery." Like the "cabinets of curiosity" popular with Europeans and Americans in the 18th and 19th centuries, books like these collected motley samples of different cultures and kinds of knowledge from all over the world and placed them in a convenient location: the almanac, the encyclopedia, the taxonomy of species, even philosophical works that aimed to gather knowledge in one place. The arrangement may seem disorderly to us, but it preserved the wonder of discovery, of multiplicity, of travel through a richly exciting landscape.

Reading *Moby-Dick*, we need to keep in mind Melville's restless and imaginative love of "curiosities" from all over the world of print and other sources. But this mode of reading and writing—browsing through a wealth of sources and collecting materials in a new form—should seem quite familiar to readers in a digital environment. Although linear reading clearly has its uses, we should not insist on it at the expense of more fluid, self-motivated, selective, and flexible modes of reading.

LOCATING MOTIVES IN *MOBY-DICK*

To recognize one's motive for reading this book, it helps to see that Melville had many motives for writing it. He had a story of danger and heroism displayed in Ahab's quest for vengeance. He wanted to convey information about whales and whaling, some derived from personal experience, some from libraries. He hoped to surpass the great masterworks of England, Europe, and the classical world by authors like Shakespeare, Milton, Rabelais, Bacon, Browne, Montaigne, Plato, Locke, and Kant. He also longed to excel as an American author, drawing on the language and themes of his own culture. He wished to make his readers laugh at the comic bewilderment of his novice whaler, Ishmael. And he wanted to take his readers on soaring flights of philosophy and fancy. He wrote in a "nervous lofty language" (*Moby-Dick*, Chapter 16) such as never had been seen before. He wanted to show places that appear on maps and also ones that are "not down on any map; true places never are" (*Moby-Dick*, Chapter 12).

Teachers might ask their students as well as themselves: Why are you reading the book? Are you interested in the story? Do you want to learn more about whales? Are you excited by the violence of the hunt? Are you fond of sailing or navigation? Are you ambitious to master a text that many people have found difficult? Each of these motives will structure one's reading experience, leading a reader to certain passages, certain destinations in the text. Your motive shapes your decisions about which signs you will heed and which you will ignore.

Similarly for Melville, different motives inspired him to use certain distinctive kinds of language, to adopt different voices that appear throughout the book. Some of Melville's voices and their different motives appear as follows.

Ishmael/The Narrator

Melville's protagonist narrates the opening chapters (1–23) continuously, and then submerges himself, often turning the action over to dramatic scenes in which he does not always appear. His voice reemerges as that of Ishmael (instead of a disembodied speaker's) in chapters like "The Mast-Head," "The Whiteness of the Whale," "The Mat-Maker," "The Town-Ho's Story," "The Monkey-Rope," "A Squeeze of the Hand," "The Try-Works," and the Epilogue. His is a genial, engaging, friendly voice, but note the omniscience of his narration, the events he describes but could not have seen. These peculiarities of his narration suggest that Ishmael wants to move fluidly through the text, that in Ishmael's voice Melville announces his freedom and power to write any way that he pleases.

The Dramatist

Melville stages certain chapters as Shakespearean scenes and soliloquies: Chapters 29–30, 36–40. (Chapter 42, "The Whiteness of the Whale," might be seen as Ishmael's soliloquy.) The Shakespearean mode, sometimes tragic, sometimes shading into comedy or melodrama, returns later in the novel in Ahab's final sections, with soliloquies by the Carpenter and Blacksmith, Ahab addressing the ocean in "The Symphony," and the men delivering final speeches in "The Chase, Third Day." These speeches and soliloquies use the archaic pronouns (*thee, thou*), sonorous rhythms, and elaborate diction of Shakespeare's plays. The voice of the dramatist suggests an aspiration toward high art, impressive language, and cultural status. In these sections, Melville seems to be competing with his literary predecessors, writing as the new American Shakespeare.

The Advocate

This voice begins in Chapter 24 ("The Advocate") and serves to defend the whalemen and their profession from detractors or explain its significance to the ignorant. It also surfaces at the end of many anatomical and technical chapters and in "The Whale as a Dish," "Jonah Historically

Regarded," and "Fast-Fish and Loose-Fish." It is passionate, political, historical, and lawyerly. Melville appears here to want to persuade a reader that his subject is important historically, economically, even mythologically.

The Preacher

Melville produces a preacher character, Father Mapple. But Ishmael adopts a sermonic voice himself in Chapter 18, "His Mark," where Bildad remarks that Ishmael gives as good a sermon as the Deacon, and later the ship's cook, Fleece, preaches in African American dialect to the sharks. Ishmael uses a preacherly tone for philosophical and symbolic thinking as well as religion, as in "The Mast-Head" or "The Try-Works." Other examples might include "The Lee Shore," "The Whiteness of the Whale," "The Mat-Maker," or "The Spirit-Spout," with the Preacher surfacing at the ends of chapters, as the Advocate sometimes does. The voice of the Preacher proclaims Melville's interest in writing a new Bible for his culture, one steeped in the idioms of working people as well as religious authorities.

The Humorist/Satirist

This figure jokes often in the opening chapters and surfaces later in a wealth of sexual humor and bawdy puns, physical slapstick and sly satire. "The Cassock" offers a sustained example, as does "Heads and Tails." Puns and wordplay break into even serious scenes. Social satire and political humor enliven chapters like "Schools and Schoolmasters," or, with more barbed effect, "Fast-Fish and Loose-Fish." As wit and satirist, Melville in this voice appears to undermine the seriousness of the religious, political, or cultural arbiters who hold sway in 19th-century society.

The Anatomist

This voice, with its scientific, rational, and encyclopedic tones, appears in "Cetology," first and foremost, and all the chapters on the whale's body. It is influenced by Darwin, Cuvier, and other biologists and comparative anatomists, as well as by practitioners of early science, as seen in medieval bestiaries and Sir Thomas Browne's *Vulgar Errors*. It can be detached, sometimes humorous, but also passionate, even bloody—offering a public dissection of the whale along with the factual information. The motive here seems to be to convince readers that, as Melville was later to say in "Billy Budd," his story is "no romance" but solid fact based on scientific observation.

The Technician

This voice appears in chapters on whaling tools and procedures, ship instruments and navigation, charts and graphs, carpentry and blacksmithing. At a certain point Ahab becomes a technician or engineer himself, as he begins rebuilding his body and refitting the ship so he can keep going. It can get geeky at times, but in his passion for the tools and weapons of whaling, the procedures and practices of its acolytes, Melville's voice as Technician takes pleasure in the process, in all its concreteness and detail.

The Poet/Artist

Ishmael often assumes this voice, from "Spirit-Spout" to the whale-as-art chapters and all over the text. This figure knows literature thoroughly and borrows from great poets and artists of the past. He chooses words for their beauty and makes up new ones; he emphasizes visual effects and scenic description. Some critics have argued that these passages scan in iambic pentameter. Melville's motive here seems to be to sweep his reader away with a vision of the beauty and power of his subject, the grand spectacle of whaling and of his characters' heroic engagement not only with the powerful whale but also with words, images, and ideas.

Once students can identify particular voices and motives (and one might come up with more than these throughout the book), they can locate places where different voices and motives intermingle in a single chapter; they might pick a chapter and see how many it contains. Students can try writing with one particular motive or convert a section that Melville has written with one motive by rewriting it with another.

OFF THE PATH, INTO THE MARGINS

Students could use a scheme like the one above to mark the text in different ways—according to certain motives that affect patterns of language or types of narration. Thus, one might pay particular attention to plot—dramatic dialogue and action, portrayals of violence, significant changes in characters' situations—and read those sections with that motive. Or one might select only the philosophical musings or lyrical outpourings or anatomy lessons or technical explanations and stick with those. Then one would be "reading with a purpose," achieving mastery of a manageable portion of the text. Such a reading might still be linear in one sense, because it would follow the shape of the novel as Melville wrote it. But it would be discontinuous, selective, and motivated in ways that would break up the linear momentum of the book.

MELVILLE'S MARGINALIA:
ANNOTATION AND ORNAMENTATION IN *MOBY-DICK*

Marking a text as above allows students to pause in reading, think about a particular passage, and respond to it. If you are reading an online text or one that you do not physically own, it is hard to scribble in the margins; underline words you especially like; or enliven the page with exclamation points, question marks, and emoticons. But Melville seldom read without a pen in hand, and the books he owned are often covered with jottings of all kinds. We encourage students to discover the pleasure of marginalia, in whatever form possible, as a way of getting off the linear path of reading and wandering in the open spaces of the margins. *Moby-Dick* offers many opportunities for annotating, commenting on, illuminating, or reshaping the text.

To get a sense of Melville's habits of annotation, go to *Melville's Marginalia Online* (Olsen-Smith, Marnon, & Norberg, n.d.). This site reproduces Melville's markings of Thomas Beale's *Natural History of the Sperm Whale* (mentioned above), as well as other volumes from Melville's personal collection. These show the many ways Melville made his texts his own, from the inscriptions on the front pages to the checks and underlinings that mark certain passages, to sometimes lengthy comments approving, or more often, violently disputing certain statements. In his copy of Beale he inscribed the title page with his own name, the date when he began reading, and the price: $3.38. Melville's annotations also show a mind reading, thinking, marking, and commenting. On a certain drawing of the whale, for example, he writes, "There is some sort of mistake. . . . The tail part is wretchedly crippled & dwarfed, & looks altogether unnatural. The head is good" (Beale, 1839, p. 33). Reading Beale's description of the whirlpool a whale makes when it dives, Melville writes, "White and green vortex in the blue—as when a ship sinks" (Beale, 1839, p. 45). He marks many details that inform passages in *Moby-Dick*, including notes for plot points that he later rejected—a scene, for example, in which Peleg, the Quaker captain, appears at sea.

Melville's *Moby-Dick* also gives examples of his habits of noting, annotating, and commenting on information, images, and ideas. The chapters "The Whiteness of the Whale" and "The Town-Ho's Story" contain footnotes; the one on the albatross in "The Whiteness of the Whale" goes on at great length and includes personal reminiscences and literary allusions. Sometimes he will insert a chapter as if to elucidate a point, or comment on something that came before or is about to come. So, for example, at the beginning of Chapter 60, "The Line," he explains, "With reference to the whaling scene shortly to be described, as well as for the better understanding of all similar scenes elsewhere presented, I have here to speak of the magical, sometimes horrible whale-line." Or, at the beginning of Chapter 83, "Jonah Historically Regarded," he goes back to pick up a detail from the previous one: "Reference was made to the historical story of Jonah and the whale in the preceding chapter." Chapter 53, "The Gam," sets up "The Town-Ho's Story" with a thorough definition of an unfamiliar term—*gam*, or social meeting between ships—and an explanation that prepares for the extraordinary events in the next chapter.

Most of these comments or even whole chapters do not add anything to the plot and have been included with the other non-plot elements, like the chapters on cetology, technical equipment, and navigation, in readers' denunciations of the book. But if we think of them as annotations they offer a different kind of experience. Like the beautiful and detailed scenes that illuminated the texts of medieval books, bringing a powerful visual dimension to the text, these moments in *Moby-Dick* invite us off the path of the plot. Here we wander in another world—sometimes contemplating a piece of scrimshaw or a painting, at other times meditating on odd questions like, What does whale meat taste like? Melville seems in one sense to have anticipated every possible annotation or footnote his subject inspires, but in another sense he invites the reader to respond to an endless array of tasty tidbits. If we think of the book as one part story and three parts marginalia, it starts to look more like the multimedia texts and multi-user domains described elsewhere in this book. And anyone can play.

Wandering off the path, then, allows a student to engage with a wide range of interests and experiences and lends itself to a devious-cruising reading of the text. One can read *Moby-Dick* from beginning to end. But remember how *Moby-Dick* begins. "Call me Ishmael"? No: "Etymology," a devious cruise through the names for *whale* in a dozen different languages, and "Extracts," a commonplace book in which are collected all the references Melville could find to whales and whaling in literature over the previous millennia. From the start, Melville invites students to wander in a world of texts and signs, picking a path that proceeds from their own hearts and minds and encouraging them to embellish the margins with their own designs.

Part III

LEARNING THROUGH REMIXING

CHAPTER 10

Is It Appropriate to Appropriate?

Henry Jenkins

The process of digitization—that is, the converting of sounds, texts, and images (both still and moving) into digital bytes of information—has paved the way for more and more of us to create new works by manipulating, appropriating, transforming, and recirculating existing media content. Such processes are becoming accessible to more and more people, including many teenagers, as tools that support music sampling or video editing are more widely available at ever lower prices. A new aesthetic based on remixing and repurposing media content has flowed across the culture—from work done by media professionals in Hollywood or artists working in top museums to teenagers mashing up their favorite anime series on their home computers or hip-hop DJs mixing and matching musical elements across different genres. The rise of digital media has also facilitated new forms of cheating, with students finding previously written papers online and turning them in as their own work, and surveillance, with teachers using digital tools to identify papers that may be plagiarized. All this has led to greater confusion over appropriate and inappropriate forms of appropriation.

Owen Gallagher, a 20-something who runs Totalrecut.com, suggests that his generation's embrace of remix practices may go back to the nursery floor:

> My brother and I were the proud owners of many *Star Wars* figures and vehicles, *Transformers, Thundercats, MASK, He-Man, G.I. Joe, Action Man* and a whole host of other toys from various movies and TV shows. Our games always consisted of us combining these different realities and storylines, mixing them up and making up our own new narratives. It

was not unusual to have Optimus Prime fighting side by side with Luke Skywalker against Mumm-Ra and Skeletor. So, from a very early age it seemed completely normal for me to combine the things I loved in new ways that seemed entertaining to me. I think that my generation and those younger than me have grown up expecting this sort of interaction with their media, on their own terms (Jenkins, 2008b).

Such early play experiences taught contemporary youth how to transform elements from popular media into resources of their own fantasy, play, and creative expression. As they have embraced new digital tools, they have been able to manipulate this source material with equal ease.

ORIGINAL USES OF BORROWED MATERIALS

Most forms of human creative expression have historically built on borrowed materials, tapping a larger cultural "reservoir" or "commons" understood to be shared by all. Our contemporary focus on "originality" as a measurement of creativity is relatively new (largely a product of the Romantic era) and relatively local (much more the case in the West than in other parts of the world). This ideal of "originality" didn't exist in the era of ancient bards, out of which sprang the works of Homer; historians who work on oral culture tell us that bards composed by drawing heavily on stories and characters already familiar to their listeners and often built up their oral epics from fragments of language shared by many storytellers (Lord, 2000). The ideal of "originality" only partially explains the works of someone like Shakespeare, who drew on the material of other playwrights and fiction writers for plots, characters, themes, and turns of phrase. Elizabeth Eisenstein, an important historian of print culture, has called our attention to a medieval text that offered four different conceptions of the author, none of which presumed totally original creation:

A man might write the works of others, adding and changing nothing, in which case he is simply called a "scribe" (*scriptor*). Another writes the work of others with additions which are not his own; and he is called a "compiler" (*compilator*). Another writes both others' work and his own, but with others' work in principal place, adding his own for purposes of explanation; and he is called a "commentator" (*commentator*). . . . Another writes both his own work and others' but with his own work in principal place adding others' for purposes of confirmation; and such a man should be called an "author" (*auctor*) (Saint Bonaventura as quoted in Eisenstein, 1979, p. 85).

Our focus on autonomous creative expression falsifies the actual process by which meaning gets generated and new works get produced. Many core works of the Western canon emerged through a process of retelling and elaboration: The figure of King Arthur goes from an obscure footnote in an early chronicle into the full-blown text of *Le Morte d'Arthur* in a few centuries, as the original story gets built upon by many generations of storytellers. None of these authors saw what they wrote as the starting point in a creative process, rather, acknowledging inspirations and influences from the past. And none of them saw what they wrote as the end point of a creative process, recognizing that their characters, stories, words, and images would be taken up by subsequent generations of creators. In fact, there were more than 200 alternative versions of *Alice in Wonderland* published commercially in the 20 years following the book's original release, including important first or early works by a number of significant children's book writers and including versions that used Wonderland's denizens to express everything from support for women's suffrage to opposition to socialism. Carolyn Sigler (1997) has argued that this quick and widespread appropriation helped to cement the book's place as one of the most oft-quoted works in the English language.

So, we are making two seemingly contradictory claims here: first, that the digital era has refocused our attention on the expressive potential of borrowing and remixing, expanding who gets to be an author and what counts as authorship; but second, that this new model of authorship is not that radical when read against a larger backdrop of human history, though it flies in the face of some of the most persistent myths about creative genius and intellectual property that have held sway since the Romantic era. Both ideas are important to communicate to students. We need to help them to understand the growing centrality of remix practices to our contemporary conception of creative expression, and we need to help them to understand how modern remix relates to much older models of authorship.

Neil Gaiman is a storyteller famous for reworking classic myths, folktales, and fairy tales, whether in the form of comics (*The Sandman* series), novels (*American Gods*), films (*Beowulf*), or television series (*Neverwhere*). During an interview, Gaiman asserted, "We have the right, and the obligation, to tell old stories in our own ways, because they are our stories" (quoted in Bender, 1999, p. xi). This statement offers an interesting starting point for talking with students about appropriation. In what sense does a culture have a "right" to retell stories that are part of its traditions? In what sense are they "our stories" rather than the legal property of the people who first created them? After all, much contemporary discussion of copyright starts from an assumption that authors have rights, while readers do not. Gaiman's statement pushes us further, though, since he asserts not simply a "right" but also an "obligation." In other words, retelling these old stories for contemporary audiences is a way of keeping their influence alive within the culture. It is something we owe the past—to carry their ideas forward into the next generation. As we retell these stories, we necessarily change them, adding or extracting elements in order to emphasize those themes that matter most to our listeners, much as an ancient bard would expand or compress a particular telling of a story depending on listener response.

In this book, we are using Herman Melville and Ricardo Pitts-Wiley as two examples of artists who create through remixing existing cultural materials, yet it is important to recognize that the same would be true, to some degree, of any novelist or director/writer we looked at. Adaptations run the gamut from highly literal-minded and faithful works, which seek to retain as much of the original as possible, to more radical transformations, which seek to recontextualize the original materials to make some new statement. Pitts-Wiley's *Moby-Dick: Then and Now* shows how the same work might combine both strategies: being very faithful to Melville's characters, plots, and language in its historical version and being highly appropriative and transformative in the contemporary version. Literary critic Kamilla Elliott has challenged what she sees as the "psychic" conception of adaptation, which assumes that the "spirit of the text" must be carried forward no matter what, suggesting instead a range of other productive metaphors through which we may understand adaptations as generating new and timely meanings through their decisions to alter or revise key aspects of the original (2004, pp. 222–223). As such, this emerging conception of adaptation is much closer to contemporary notions of remix and mashup than might otherwise be imagined.

FROM ALLUSION TO SAMPLING

Although they don't use the terminology, literature teachers have already been trained to think about sampling and remix practices: They often teach about a writer's sources of inspiration. The new emphasis on remix culture among contemporary youth may provide teachers an opportunity to revitalize some concepts central to their discipline and to talk with students about cultural practices that are part of their own everyday experience. When speaking about literature, we tend to talk about allusions, while in discussing contemporary music, we talk about sampling. Both can be modest—a few words in the case of a literary allusion or a few chords in the case of a music sample. The term *allusion* stresses the conceptual links between two works, while *sampling* stresses the borrowing of materials, but both are ways of referring to how a new author may extract elements from or pay tribute to an existing work as part of his or her attempts to shape the meanings or emotional impact of the work. For our purposes, we are using allusion and sampling as if they were more or less equivalent concepts. The sample is the material borrowed from the other work, while *the remix* refers to the new work created through this process of appropriation and recombination. In the lingo of contemporary music, a *mashup* would refer to the combination of two or more works to create something new, while a *remix* would refer to a work that combines borrowed and original materials.

Seeing sampling as another way into thinking about allusion suggests answers to questions we often receive from teachers: How can you tell if a remix is good? How can you tell if an allusion is good? An allusion is good when it is generative, when it extends the original work's potential meaningfulness, when it taps the power of the original source to add new depth to your emotional experience of the current work. The same claims would hold true for other kinds of remix practices: As a general rule, a remix is valuable if it is generative and meaningful rather than arbitrary and superficial.

A Note About Plagiarism and Infringement

Renee Hobbs's *Copyright Clarity: How Fair Use Supports Digital Learning* is an important guide for teachers seeking to understand the complex set of ethical, legal, and creative issues surrounding remix culture. Hobbs, a longtime media literacy scholar and educator who examined classroom practices around copyright and remix for the MacArthur Foundation, writes:

> Plagiarism is using someone else's work without attribution. We think of plagiarism as "cut and paste" writing. . . . Although the conduct of plagiarism may overlap with copyright infringement, the two concepts are distinct. You can plagiarize from Shakespeare, but you'll never have a copyright problem, since his works are in the public domain. Plagiarism is an ethical problem handled by teachers and schools; copyright infringement is a legal problem handled by the courts. (2010, p. 8)

We might extend her argument here: Remix and allusion are aesthetic practices having to do with referencing other people's creative works as part of your own expressive practices. A remix may or may not be authorized, may be from a work that falls into public domain, may fall within fair use, may constitute a form of critical engagement that is protected by the law, and thus may or may not be infringement. A remix may also acknowledge or mask its sources and thus may or may not be plagiarism. But ultimately, it should be judged on the basis of its creative contributions—what it adds to the meanings associated with the original work, how it deploys those meanings to create something new. The use of mechanical tools to ferret out plagiarists contributes to the confusion, since they can tell whether a piece of text is being reused, but not the conditions under which it is being used. In that sense, they do not in and of themselves help you to separate infringement, plagiarism, and remix in meaningful ways. For this reason, "zero tolerance" policies that categorically punish the use of other people's materials are profoundly unhelpful in preparing students for a world where we use other people's content all the time, but there are legal, ethical, and aesthetic stakes in the choices we make in relation to other people's content.

MC LARS'S "AHAB": DISSECTING A REMIX

Before we deal with the complex series of appropriations and transformations that shape Pitts-Wiley's *Moby-Dick: Then and Now*, it might be helpful to refine our vocabulary by looking at a relatively simpler remix of Melville's novel, the music video that nerdcore performer MC Lars developed for his song "Ahab" (MC Lars, 2006). Analysis is intended to model a basic set of questions that can be asked about any remix or adaptation and help us to identify the ways it expands the meanings associated with the original.

What Constitutes the Primary Source Material?

Like many examples of remix, the song combines its primary source—*Moby-Dick*—with other allusions. "Ahab" evokes contemporary reference points that would have been anachronistic in Melville's novels, such as Steve Wozniak, the Mariana Trench, *Titanic*, and *Finding Nemo* (suggested by the clown fish at the end of the video). A tossed-off reference to "a Supergrass beat" acknowledges another group whose music MC Lars samples for this song. Remix often gets described as "plagiarism"; yet, in fact, it can be seen as the opposite of plagiarism: Plagiarists usually seek to cover their tracks, masking the sources of their material and taking claim for them.

Remix, on the other hand, depends on our recognition that the material is being borrowed and often depends on our understanding of the specific contexts it is borrowed from (suggesting a logic closer to allusions than to plagiarism). This song would be meaningless if we did not recognize its references to Herman Melville. And it says something about the ethics within this community that the songwriter acknowledges the beats he sampled.

What Is the Media Form of the Remix?

Moby-Dick was a printed novel; *Ahab* was a music video distributed primarily through YouTube.

What Is the Context of the Remix?

MC Lars, along with Sir Frontalot, mc chris, Optimus Rhyme, and Baddd Spellah, is widely considered a founder of the so-called nerdcore movement. *Nerdcore* refers to a subgenre of hip-hop music whose themes and images are drawn from geek interests: games, science and science fiction, computers and digital culture, and cult media in particular. For example, consider his video for "Space Game," which not only celebrates early arcade games but also makes references to characters from *Star Wars* (Darth Maul, Boba Fett, Sith girls, etc.), *Lost in Space* (Dr. Smith), classic *Star Trek* (Captain Kirk, Scotty, Spock), *Star Trek: The Next Generation* (Q, The Borg), *2001: A Space Odyssey* (Hal), *The Matrix* (Neo and Morpheus), *X-Men* (Magneto), *Superman* (Zod), and even Dr. Seuss ("The Obleck"). In later verses, the song lays claim to being "postmodernist" (under the banner of Robert Ventura and Andy Warhol) and ridicules modernists such as T. S. Eliot, Ezra Pound, Virginia Woolf, Joseph Conrad, Franz Kafka, e. e. cummings, Wallace Stevens, and Frank Lloyd Wright. Watching this video with your students may be a good way to help them understand how allusion creates a juncture between old and new stories and in this case, between high art and popular culture.

Several of MC Lars's songs, including "iGeneration" and "Download This Song," constitute manifestos for those who have grown up in a world where music is easy to access and where remix is part of what it means to consume popular culture. "Ahab" was one of several songs MC Lars based on canonical literary works; he reads with the same playful irreverence with which he approaches icons of science fiction culture. "RapBeth" represents his hip-hop ode to William Shakespeare, while "Mr. Raven" signals his respect for Edgar Allan Poe. MC Lars has a degree in English literature from Oxford University and has said that he would have pursued a career as an English teacher if he hadn't found success as a hip-hop performer.

What Elements of the Primary Source Material Are Being Remixed?

"Ahab" includes a high number of reference points to the novel, some of which are expressed through the lyrics (such as the reference to the gold doubloon Ahab nails to the mast or the shout-out to Queequeg), some through the visual iconography (for example, the scar on Ahab's face or his peg leg). The line "Hey Ishmael . . . can I call you annoying?" plays upon "Call me Ishmael," probably the single most famous phrase in Melville's novel. The repeated chorus, "Peg leg, sperm whale, jaw bone, what!" not only refers to some of the recurring icons of the narrative but also hints at the novel's linkage of Ahab's leg with the ivory of the whale. The conflict between Ahab and Starbuck is implied by "You're never going to find him! He's a big sperm whale. The ocean is enormous!" while other lines point to Ahab's self-absorption and solitude: "Excuse me while I go be melancholy in my room!" Another lyric neatly captures a key subplot in the novel: "Pip went insane when he almost drowned, So profound when he shrieks like a little sailor clown." The visual logic of the video, which takes us underwater and then into the mouth and through the belly of the whale, evokes the story of Jonah, who is swallowed by a great fish, which Melville reads as a whale, while the hectoring figure in the turban here may suggest Elijah's warning or Fedallah's prophecy.

MC Lars is able to shorthand *Moby-Dick* because so many of his listeners will already know the story through other media representations, if not through a direct experience of the book. MC Lars simply has to point us in the right direction, and our mind fills in all the rest, with much of the humor here stemming from the brevity with which he is able to sum up such a vast and intimidating work.

Are the Works of the Same or Different Genre? How Do You Know?

Moby-Dick is a literary epic with tragic overtones; "Ahab" is a music video with comic overtones.

What Techniques Are Deployed in Reworking the Original Material?

The song compresses the complex and lengthy novel into a series of evocative phrases. "Ahab" relies on anachronisms to hint at the relationship between past and present. The song incorporates key phrases from literary analysis to suggest a particular set of interpretations of the novel. The staging of the music video is intended to evoke a school pageant, hinting at the relationship of this text to secondary education. The song's bouncy beat transforms the tone and spirit of the original book, inviting us to have fun with *Moby-Dick* rather than taking it totally seriously.

What Is the Intended Purpose of the Remix?

"Ahab" is a good-natured parody, one that deflates the elevated reputation of the original novel, even as it acknowledges its continued relevance. The song may be harsher toward some of the ways novels get taught through schools. Like several of MC Lars's other songs, "Ahab" blurs the line between high art and popular culture, suggesting an ongoing criticism of cultural hierarchies.

How Does the Remix Build on, Add to, or Alter the Cultural Meaning of the Original Work?

The song suggests some of the interpretations of *Moby-Dick* that arise in high school literature classes. Ahab describes himself as a "monomaniac," draws parallels to Oedipus, talks about "hubris" as his "tragic flaw," defines the book's conflict as "man vs. beast," and sums up the book's message as "revenge is never sweet." All this is the stuff of SparkNotes, suggesting a work that may come pre-digested, neatly broken down into familiar modes of analysis.

That "Ahab" is responding to the rituals of the English classroom is further hinted at through the visuals, which depict students reenacting *Moby-Dick*, and end with a shot from the wings as the performance concludes and the audience applauds. The nerdcore movement tends to embrace low-tech and amateur-looking graphics in many videos, hinting at the do-it-yourself culture that inspires them and their audiences. Ironically, here, the stagecraft is more elaborate than would likely be seen in any school pageant, making, perhaps, a reference to the spectacular and equally unlikely high school productions of films like *Apocalypse Now* depicted in the cult classic *Rushmore*. The video is a thumbing of the nose at the practices of secondary education, even as it is also an affectionate tribute to the novel itself.

REMIX PRACTICES IN RICARDO PITTS-WILEY'S *MOBY-DICK*: THEN AND NOW

Ricardo Pitts-Wiley, his cast, and his crew mirror a mode of reading that is at once intensive, looking closely at Melville's text, and extensive, searching constantly for the wider contexts in which *Moby-Dick* operates, the sources it drew upon, and the more recent texts that have reacted to its provocations and inspirations. In that way, *Moby-Dick: Then and Now* helps us to understand more fully the ways that remix practices draw upon the habit of close reading. Ricardo Pitts-Wiley tells us that remix starts from a "respect" for the original, from readers trying to understand as fully as possible what the author was trying to say and trying to iden- tify the historical contexts that shaped the work being sampled; remix also involves a creative re-envisioning and repurposing of the original, recognizing hidden potentials in the material that may become clear only when it is juxtaposed with ideas and images borrowed from elsewhere. Remix doesn't preserve the purity of the original, but it does grow out of a creative and insightful engagement with what comes before. This re- spectful reading is what distinguishes a rich and meaningful remix from one that is superficial.

Close Reading: Alba and Pip

We might start with a basic example, which suggests just how com- plexly Pitts-Wiley's remix practices operate in relation to the dramatic structure of the play. The scene involves Alba, the young Asian Ameri- can woman who stands in for Ahab in the contemporary setting, and her younger brother, Pip. The opening sequence of the play tells us that Pip has been killed in a drive-by shooting, and as the story unfolds, we learn more about the circumstances leading up to his death.

Pip is portrayed as a book-smart kid, someone who spends time in the library reading up about whatever interests him, a characterization relying on clichés running through many contemporary works dealing with Black street life (e.g., *Boyz n the Hood* or *The Wire*, season 4) where the family seeks, often unsuccessfully, to protect intellectual siblings from being exposed to the dangers and corruptions of life in the 'hood. The name Pip, of course, already resonates for readers of Melville's novel, since Pip is the young cabin boy whom the crew was unable to protect; the boy is driven insane when he is left adrift, by himself, as a consequence of being thrown overboard during a struggle with a whale. Pip's dialogue evokes the fate of the character in Melville's novel when Pip describes his thoughts as a rival gang is shooting up his house: "I thought I was going to go crazy. I was just going crazy, crazy scared. I thought I saw God. I was crazy dreaming just waiting for them to find me. But they didn't. You came back and saved me."

In this scene, the two worlds come together: Pip's bookishness is suggested by his excitement over learning about cetology at school, and his sister's destructive environment is suggested by his repeated questions about why she locks him away in the house rather than letting him participate in the gang's deals.

The exchange between Pip and his sister about cetology compresses into a few paragraphs the dense and detailed description of whale biology found in *Moby-Dick*. At one point, Pip interrupts his lecture with "Am I boring you?", a playful acknowledgment of the frustration some contemporary readers feel with the level of detail found in such passages. That Pip is interested in this whaling lore suggests, in fact, that there is not as big a disconnect between the contemporary and historical sections as we might imagine and sets us up to draw further parallels between the dangers confronting the gangs and those affecting the ship's crew.

This speech also sets up a key line, "If you ever out whale hunting, don't worry about the head, watch out for the tail," a line that resurfaces at the end of the play, when Pip reappears, offering advice to his sister that allows her and the One to turn back from the destruction that befell Ahab and his crew: "Go home. Get him out of your lives. Out of the hood. He doesn't stay where strong people live." These allusions to *Moby-Dick* do complex work: helping to establish the relationship between Alba and Pip, helping to build a bridge between the historic and contemporary settings, helping to foreshadow the alternative ending of the story, and acknowledging some of the aspects of the book that had to be cut out for the stage play.

Yet Pitts-Wiley also deploys allusions to contemporary popular culture here. Immediately before this scene, Que, Alba's right-hand guy, sums up what happened to Pip: "He thought he could be better at the game then us. He thought he could play a little game with WhiteThing. It was just a game from a boy that Alba tried to save. Game over." The image of drug dealing as a "game" is a well-trodden metaphor, but the closing phrase, "game over" references the conventions of computer and video games. Suddenly, we read the earlier reference to Alba's attempt to "save" Pip not simply through a language of salvation but also in terms of a video game where players can "save" a well-played game and return to it again in the future.

Critics of video games note that this ability to save games takes away some of the sting of death, making it hard for games to depict real tragedy, since no character remains permanently dead; one can simply reboot and play again. Here, Que's "game over" carries a finality that helps to motivate much of the other action in the play. It is precisely because Alba cannot reboot and return to a world where her little brother is still alive and protected from the terrors of WhiteThing that she is later forced to break out of the game she has been playing and follow a different set of rules. Here, again, the language prepares us for the final moment of the play where the One reverse course, rejecting revenge as a way of dealing with their problems, and imagining an alternative life for themselves in the future.

Allusions to Popular Culture

Pitts-Wiley's play merges multiple bodies of knowledge, making allusions to elements of Melville's original novel and deploying references to contemporary popular culture. Some teachers are going to feel more comfortable teasing out the literary references here, but keep in mind that the popular culture references will allow your students to share some of their mastery and expertise. Historically, such knowledge of popular culture gets dismissed as trivia and is often deflected from classroom discussions, yet when we do this we communicate two things to students: that the things they know outside school have no relevance inside school and that the things they learn in school may also be irrelevant to what they do with the rest of their lives. Both these messages are destructive to the pedagogical process. Teachers need to be willing to suspend judgment and allow young people to draw on their knowledge of popular culture to decipher *Moby-Dick: Then and Now*, much as Pitts-Wiley learned to trust his young actors to add more swagger to his language.

One important step will be to have students go through the play and see how many different references and allusions they can identify. Then, have them do a little research—online, in the library, take your pick, though they will probably need to do some of both if they are going to dig out everything they need to know so they can process some of these analogies. Wikipedia may be more useful for understanding the references to popular culture than an encyclopedia or other traditional reference works.

In the notes that follow, we will trace some of the more interesting allusions found in this particular performance, though there is no way we can exhaust them in this chapter. As you think about these references, remember the many different levels on which a stage play operates, each of which offers potential openings through which to remix or reference existing works: the written language of the play, the setting, the costumes, the performances, the soundtrack. In what follows, we have chosen examples that work with many different properties of theater as a mode of expression.

"Compared to Him, We Just Nemo"

Here, Que makes probably the most explicit connection in the play between Moby Dick and WhiteThing, keeping in mind the slipperiness in Melville between whether a whale is a fish or a mammal, a slipperiness that emerges in part from his constant deployment of the biblical story of Jonah, who was swallowed by a "great fish." This comparison is further complicated by the reference to Nemo, the protagonist of the Disney/Pixar animated feature *Finding Nemo*. There are two sequences in the film that pit the small fish—in this case, Nemo's father, Marlin, and his friend, Dory—against a big WhiteThing: First (scene 8 on the DVD) Marlin and Dory find themselves in the midst of a gathering of sharks, dominated by a great white shark named Bruce. (Bruce was actually the nickname used for the robotic shark that Steven Spielberg's production company used in filming *Jaws*, a film that helped cement the great white shark as an object of fear in our collective imagination.) *Finding Nemo* uses the sharks to parody 12-step programs designed to overcome addictions; in this case, the sharks are bonding together to try to overcome their desires to eat smaller fish ("Fish are friends, not food"). Later in the film, Dory tries to communicate with a whale (scene 19), which ultimately swallows them, transports them to Sydney, and ejects them through its spout in a scene that might recall the story of Jonah (scene 21) but also the Disney version of *Pinocchio*. Here, the film offers compelling imagery of the immense scale of the whale, especially seen from the perspective of a much smaller fish. Here's what Pitts-Wiley had to say about this sequence in my correspondence with him:

> I love the line because it speaks to their [the young gang members'] ultimate innocence. I never had to explain that line to any of those people, anybody who heard it, particularly in their own age group. They knew instantly what that meant. *Finding Nemo* is in their world,

it's part of the vernacular, and very efficient. . . . I wish I could take credit for it, but the kids came up with that line.

Daj's *Scarface* T-Shirt

Susan Bergeron, the costume designer for the production, encouraged the young actors to find their own clothes for their characters, feeling that they were going to be closer to the youth cultures depicted in the play. In everyday life, we read T-shirts as personal statements, which signal to the world our political beliefs, personal philosophies, or cultural preferences. In this case, the *Scarface* shirt does this and a bit more. The 1983 *Scarface* film, with Al Pacino, was a remake of the 1932 gangster drama of the same title. While the Depression-era version depicted Scarface as an Italian American immigrant caught up in the era of gangsters brought about by Prohibition, the 1983 version depicted a Cuban American gang leader, who rises to power through his control over the sale of cocaine. Something of the values associated with this character is hinted at by the subtitles of the two recent video games based on the *Scarface* saga: "The World Is Yours" and "Money. Power. Respect." We can compare that message with Stu's statement about the values that drive the One: "White powder to green cash. Cash to power. The power to live like we want to live." In the film, the protagonist is ultimately gunned down in an act of gangland vengeance for his refusal to murder a congressman who threatens to uncover the drug trade. One can read *Scarface*, then, as a modern tragedy about a megalomaniac who is brought down by the logic of vengeance that shapes the entire drug culture: Ironically, it is the crime he refuses to commit rather than the many he does that brings about his tragic fall. Pitts-Wiley notes:

> If you are age 30 to 60, the number one movie of the last 50 years is *The Godfather*. If you are age 12 to 40, *Scarface* is number one. Why are *The Godfather* and *Scarface* so much a part of pop culture in this country? They both so fit into the American mythological idea of itself. We admire Vito Corleone because he said, "I'll do it my way. That's the American way. I'm gonna do it the way I do it. I'm not gonna play by the rules." Tony Montana says, "I'm coming to the land of opportunity and I'm going to live it to its fullest. I'm gonna do it my way. I'm gonna live hard, I'm gonna live fast, and I'll die hard if I have to. But on the way, I'm gonna live like a prince," and young people identify with that. . . . We love that, that independent spirit, individualism. Take advantage

of opportunity, grow, grow wealthy, control your own destiny. . . . They talk about it in the play: "We do it our way. We don't flip hamburgers, we don't wait in line, we live hard and we live fast." But you know there's a horrible part of it because Que opens his monologue by saying, "In my neighborhood, nobody expects to live for a long time." You know in the whaling industry, nobody expected to live for a long time. They're the same thing.

"Grand Contested Election . . ."

Both Ishmael in the historical setting and Stu in the modern setting are reading a text describing developments that seem contemporary to many viewers: "Grand contested election for the presidency of the United States. Bloody battle in Afghanistan." In fact, the text is taken from a playbill referenced by Melville in Chapter 1, "Loomings." In the original, Melville included a third act, "Whaling Voyage by one Ishmael," situated between the other two, a hint at what is to come and an acknowledgment that Ishmael, at least, will survive the destruction of the ship. Even as we see the same references unfold across both time periods, Stu underlines the connection by mumbling, "I swear, if it wasn't for the sports section, the news would be the same every day." This passage of Melville's has gained new relevance in the wake of the 2000 elections and 9/11 and its aftermath, suggesting a way of reading *Moby-Dick: Then and Now* as a political allegory.

Rick Benjamin, who was originally Pitts-Wiley's creative partner on this production, wanted the play to be a much more overt critique of the Bush administration, and the artists parted company over this issue. One can find some traces of that political allegory at play here, especially as we watch the drama between Ahab, determined to follow a path of revenge even though he knows it brings about his own destruction, and Starbuck, who knows Ahab must be stopped and yet lacks the will to stand up to the powerful figure. Some have read this confrontation as similar to the inability of the Democratic Congress to exert sufficient will and political force to block George W. Bush's entry into the war in Iraq. This reading is consistent with a number of recent editorial cartoons, which have used the image of Ahab's quest for the great white whale to comment on Bush's pursuit of the war on terror. Even in the absence of an explicit political allegory, the headlines signal how many of the same issues were being confronted in the world Melville depicted as in our own, including uncertainties about the nature of power and about justifications for war. Pitts-Wiley explains:

The parallels between Melville's time and ours tell us that we will always be involved in political struggle. Unless we change our national identity and profile we're always going to be engaged in some type of conflict with somebody else, somewhere in the world. Afghanistan today, Iraq tomorrow, China the day after. . . . Sometimes I think Melville's clearly saying that's what we are as people—otherwise he wouldn't have written in so much detail about the politics of the ship. The first mate sits here, he's first; the second mate cannot sit down until the first mate has sat down and eaten; the third mate can't sit down until the second mate has sat down; and if you're the third or the second mate you're really in a bad way because when the first mate is finished eating that means you're finished eating, too, because when he gets up you get up. That's just politics and power, and power-play politics that makes you aspire to be in a more powerful position regardless of your ability: You just want to eat better.

Teen Idol

Teen Idol is a composite of many contemporary youth stars: the reference to "Idol" serves double duty, both referring to the popular *American Idol* series and suggesting the concept of idolatry as false worship. Through Teen Idol, Pitts-Wiley hints at the glamorization of violence and drug culture in popular entertainment. Teen Idol warns Alba, "Don't believe everything that you read about me," and worries that Alba notices the "fine guys" (his bodyguards) at poolside when he wants to stress his heterosexual prowess ("They're only supposed to let pretty girls in"). When he's asked directly whether his real life matches his gangster image, he first tries to bluff ("Livin' the hardcore life"), then points toward the way his image gets taken up by aspirational fans ("Showing my fans how they could live if they could only get to the promised land"), and then finally acknowledging, "My manager and my record company tell me that getting caught with a little blow is good for business." Elsewhere, he concedes, however, that as a pop star, he is exempt from many of the penalties his fans would face if they were caught using the same drugs ("Stars don't do time. We do 'rehab.'").

Later, we see Teen Idol singing a song that mashes up a range of other pop songs, including The Eagles' "Hotel California," Jimi Hendrix's "Purple Haze," and America's "A Horse with No Name," all three of which reference contemporary drug culture. The intermingling of the lines suggests both the recycling of familiar themes and beats in contemporary pop music and the recurrence of pro-drug messages in much contemporary culture. "A Horse with No Name" and "Hotel California" also both point toward lonely and ultimately aimless journeys from which the protagonist has little or no chance of returning, themes that resonate with the plot of *Moby-Dick.* Consider how the line "They stab it with their steely knives but they just can't kill the beast," evokes Ahab's battle with the whale, regardless of what those lines mean in the context of "Hotel California."

Here's how Pitts-Wiley discusses the figure of Teen Idol:

> If you're a pop star—and this has been true for a long time—[you] get busted and get away with it. You don't fail down, you fail up. . . . The bigger the star, the bigger the drugs. That's why "Purple Haze," "acting funny and I don't know why, excuse me while I kiss the sky." So much of our music of the time was about getting high, flying out. Go to the "Horse With No Name." "Been through the desert on a horse with no name. It felt good to be out of the rain. In the desert you can't remember your name, 'cause there ain't no one to give you no pain." When I grew up somebody had to tell me about "cloud nine." This was The Temptations; this was the name of their album, *Cloud Nine.* The childhood part of my life wasn't very pretty. I was born and raised in the heart of the city. But I'm doing fine on cloud nine. You can be what you want to be. You ain't got no responsibility. Every man in his mind is free. (Temptations lyrics paraphrased by Pitts-Wiley.)

So, in the example above, we have included allusions that get communicated through dialogue ("Cetology," "Game Over"), costume (the *Scarface* T-shirt), and music (Teen Idol's song). Many of the allusions to popular culture point in the same direction—toward the ways street gangs and drugs get depicted, often glamorized, by contemporary media. Underlying those references, then, is a critique of the entertainment media as part of the complex system of economic, social, cultural, and political relationships the play calls WhiteThing. WhiteThing exerts its power over us in many ways, but among them, it reshapes the contents of our imagination, creating fantasies of power and wealth (whether the spectacular consumption in *Scarface* or the consciousness-altering power of drugs depicted in Teen Idol's song and celebrity image), and marketing expensive brands to poor consumers that force them to step outside the law to remain competitive (as in Soccer Mom's discussion of branded tennis shoes). The pop culture referenced here is very much part of the world inhabited by the One, by the young actors in the production, and, Pitts-Wiley hopes, by his young viewers. These references to contemporary popular culture are as central to the meaning of this work as are the allusions to Melville's original novel; they are simply designed to speak to different segments of the audience.

CHAPTER 11

Both a Borrower and a Lender Be

Wyn Kelley

This chapter looks at the creative ways classic authors recombine texts and media modalities from different sources of inspiration. As students observe how traditional authors recombine other forms, they may be likewise inspired to work creatively with the texts they encounter. Herman Melville's *Moby-Dick* provides many examples of how imaginative remixing enriches and expands the text. At the same time as he remixes, adding to and enriching his novel, Melville also leaves gaps and silences, places in the text where alert readers may supply their own narratives. The power and endurance of a classic work frequently depends on this balance between what has been added and what is left open for further elaboration. Appreciating this creative play between what a book takes and what it offers, students can find their own pathways into a novel even as diverse and sometimes bewildering as *Moby-Dick*. Creating a participatory culture in an English classroom can start with the recognition that literary texts are participatory spaces themselves.

MELVILLE AS BORROWER

This appreciation begins with an awareness of why and under what conditions a writer like Melville might engage in practices that we now find dubious, if not illegal. Students may rightly ask, and often do, why literary borrowing is seen as "creative," "imaginative," and "inspired" when Herman Melville does it but is called "plagiarism" when they remix the materials they find online. We need to take this question seriously.

Many students seem to understand the two basic points of any typical discussion of the topic. First, we have copyright laws to protect artists whose creative work might be stolen, writers whose intellectual property could be violated, scholars whose discoveries risk being purloined and exploited. Second, writers use citations to invite readers into the conversation they implicitly hold with people whose ideas they have read and reflected on in making a creative, intellectual, or scholarly work. Footnotes advertise the depth of their research (hence the common abuse of padding bibliographies), but they also acknowledge that thought does not take place in a vacuum, that it grows out of and depends on the ideas and findings of others. When we credit those sources or inspirations or mentors, we make their materials available for other readers to interpret and comment on too. In this model, creativity and scholarship resemble the ideals of democratic society, to create free access and opportunity for all.

In practice, as students all too quickly realize, the world of ideas does not always work as a free society, and scholars do not always abide by these ideals. It is disillusioning to learn, as an article at *Inside Higher Ed* (Guess, 2008) reported, that a study of citations in scientific journals revealed an extent of error and misrepresentation leading to the conclusion that authors were citing articles they could not have read. Even more common are the reports of plagiarism among well-known authors of both fiction and nonfiction, scholarly and nonscholarly work (McGrath, 2007), or even among politicians and political candidates (Zeleny, 2008). Too often literary borrowing is seen as simply theft, or as a zero-sum game, where someone's creative play robs another writer or maker of valuable creative capital.

In a text like *Moby-Dick,* however, it can become an opportunity, even an engine driving the book. Herman Melville offers a couple of ways to think about creative appropriation, a problem that in our current media environment remains open rather than completely resolved. The first is historical, the second philosophical.

The historical context for thinking about Melville's borrowing, as well as that of any author writing before the codification of copyright law in the late 19th century, suggests that the modern concept of protecting intellectual property is a relatively recent invention. When Melville began writing in the 1840s, most American authors did not automatically receive copyright protection by printing their works in the United States. They had to publish them first in England and then sell them to American printers; and even then they might see cheap pirated versions of their works being sold by other printers. In this environment, authors could not always rely on protection of their own intellectual or creative property, nor did they always observe the boundaries of other people's. Melville refers to this problem throughout *Moby-Dick*, often in oblique and humorous ways. For example, for his chapter on whales, "Cetology," he mixes materials from known whaling authorities like Thomas Beale, William Scoresby, and J. Ross Browne, along with a host of historians, scientists, and philosophers, without in general identifying his sources. Then he creates fictional authors, throws in what a few of his seafaring friends had to say, and slyly mocks the whole matter of scholarly authority itself by arranging his whales according to size, as if they were books on a shelf (folios, octavos, etc.) rather than species and genera. Such blithe disregard for the principles of scientific discourse and taxonomy, while showing more respect for the opinions of "Simeon Macey and Charley Coffin, of Nantucket" than for Linnaeus, shows how fluidly writers might borrow from sources in Melville's period. We see similar kinds of pastiche and collage in the works of Frederick Douglass, Harriet Beecher Stowe, Mark Twain, and many others throughout the 19th century.

A second, more personal and philosophical framework for thinking about how Melville viewed borrowing appears in a set of letters he exchanged with friend and fellow author Nathaniel Hawthorne (Kelley, 2008). Melville took a trip to Nantucket, where he heard the story of Agatha Hatch, a woman who rescued a shipwrecked sailor, nursed him back to health, married him, and then, when he abandoned her before the birth of a daughter, waited patiently (17 years) for his return. Melville thought Hawthorne should write the story, and he sent him the materials he would need for doing so, along with a detailed account of how Hawthorne ought to write it. Eventually Hawthorne declined, and Melville wrote the story himself, although it does not survive. At one point, in insisting that Hawthorne take up the story, Melville claimed that it was never his own; it was always Hawthorne's. "I do not therefore, My Dear Hawthorne, at all imagine that you will think that I am so silly as to flatter myself that I am giving you anything of my own. I am but restoring to you your own property— which you would have quickly enough have identified for yourself—had you but been on the spot as I happened to be" (quoted in Kelley, 2008, p. 194). Melville implies that the story belongs to Hawthorne because Hawthorne, given his writing style and interests, is the person to produce it. He also implies that literary property can travel fluidly between one author and another, between writer and reader.

Melville's "borrowing" of Agatha's story, first from the person who told it to him and then, while he pondered its details, from Hawthorne, to whom he considered that it rightfully belonged, greatly stretches our notion of literary borrowing as happening when someone simply takes details from one source and puts them, or remixes them into another work. Melville's idea of borrowing involves a creative dialogue between different writers, a collaboration between writers and readers, in an endless process in which the finished product seems secondary to the fascinating relationships that evolve along the way. This concept suggests a far less goal- and object-oriented notion of literary property than our modern notions would emphasize.

I would want students, then, to recognize that plagiarism is a somewhat narrow legal concept within a much broader and older tradition of literary, intellectual, creative, and scholarly borrowing and appropriation. It may seem hard for students to maintain two such conflicting views of borrowing at the same time. I would remind them, though, that we live with such a double awareness all the time. My father learned to drive in rural South Carolina during a time when 10-year-olds commonly drove cars. There was no legal driving age. Our traffic laws, which mandate that we observe speed limits, protect the bodies and properties of other drivers, and strive to maintain safe highways, have followed fairly recently from a period in which popular culture enshrined the automobile as an icon of speed and danger. We still live with those conflicting messages. So it should not surprise us to learn that plagiarism is bad, and at the same time that literary borrowing is a sign of creativity, and that the best writers can be the worst offenders. We can give students a way to practice these techniques themselves so that they can gain a more complex and intimate knowledge of how literary borrowing works. If nothing else, they can come away from this practice with a more sophisticated understanding of plagiarism than "It's bad."

ISHMAEL, AHAB, AND QUEEQUEG AS REMIXERS

Melville's characters offer different models of how remixing works, enlarging our sense not only of *what* an author takes from sources but also of *how* he or she recycles texts and media.

Ishmael, for example, might be called a literary *scavenger*. He shows his mastery of an endless array of authors and texts from all domains of literate culture: theology, philosophy, mythology, poetry, natural history and science, art and architecture, history, travel accounts, and maritime chronicles. In a typical example, Chapter 86 ("The Tail"), he presents himself first as a poet: "Other poets have warbled the praises of the soft eye of the antelope, and the lovely plumage of the bird that never alights; less celestial, I celebrate a tail." He proceeds, then, as an anatomist might, pulling back the skin and revealing the muscle structure and inner workings of the whale's "member." Switching to the arts to describe the awesome power of the tail, he compares it to the massive chest of Germany's greatest Romantic author, Goethe, to a Roman triumphal arch, and to one of Michelangelo's paintings. Next, adopting the technique of a scientist, he lists the five different motions of the tail, explaining each in physical detail. The chapter ends with an excursion into philosophy, as he contemplates the extraordinary expressiveness of the whale's use of his tail to signify a wide range of meanings, and he also includes a reference to the biblical Jehovah, whom the whale, in his inscrutability, seems to resemble: "Thou shalt see my back parts, my tail, he seems to say, but my face shall not be seen."

Ishmael's method involves not simply throwing a great number of allusions on the page but also flexibly adapting their characteristic discourses and strategies. The list of the whale's physical traits comes straight from the encyclopedia or textbook. Yet at the same time each scientific explanation abounds in metaphors and serves as a small poem. The concluding paragraph mocks the anatomical study: "Dissect him how I may, then, I go but skin deep." But in doing so it offers a witty philosophical twist. At the same time, it reaches for the rhetorical effect of a sermon, with its adaptation of biblical language. Ishmael's imaginative juxtapositions of various and unlike elements create poetry out of blubber, as Melville jokingly remarked in a letter to his friend Richard Henry Dana.

Whereas Ishmael displays the book's most spectacular literary virtuosity, in Ahab we find a literary *engineer*. This is not to say that Ahab does not have extraordinary literary abilities like Ishmael's. Melville gives him the most elevated Shakespearean language for his speeches and soliloquies, which borrow flourishes from classical oratory and sermonic diction as well. But Ahab shows his greatest creative power in the way he adapts materials for new purposes. In particular, he cuts whalebone to size and fits it to his thigh to replace the leg Moby Dick sheared away. When the bone breaks he has a new leg made and contemplates replacing other parts of himself one by one. Some readers have seen in Ahab's image of ideal man made to order, a kind of cyborg or Frankensteinian creation. Just as much as he tinkers with his body, Ahab also shows considerable mechanical genius in the way he fixes broken equipment or finds handy replacements for lost instruments (Chapters 24 and 25, "The Needle" and "The Log and Line"). With Ahab, then, Melville presents a practical form of adaptation or repurposing, that makes effective use of available materials for new uses. As with his physical materials, Ahab adapts nautical charts, whaling histories, bloody rituals, theatrical performances, and the language of power and command to weld his men into a machine that can hunt and kill the great whale.

A third model of creative adaptation, Queequeg the harpooneer, might be called a *cultural migrant*. Queequeg must continually adapt the customs, tools, and texts of his new (American) culture to his own (Polynesian) framework, just as he translates his particular rituals and talents to a new sphere. Ishmael mocks such oddities as Queequeg's putting his clothes on—hat first, then boots (under the bed), finally pantaloons (Chapter 4, "The Counterpane"). But Queequeg laughs at American customs when he makes fun of a Yankee captain who treats a ceremonial punch bowl at an island feast as a finger bowl, washing his hands in the "blessed beverage" (Chapter 13, "Wheelbarrow").

Queequeg's abilities as translator and adaptor reveal themselves often throughout the book, most notably in his success as a whaleman. At a later point, however, he also adapts and moves texts around when, thinking he is about to die, he orders his coffin built; when he unexpectedly recovers, he converts the coffin into a sea chest and engraves it with designs copied from the tattooings all over his body. Ishmael recognizes that these mystical symbols, derived from sacred images engraved on Queequeg's skin, represent "a complete theory of the heavens and the earth, and a mystical treatise on the art of attaining truth" (Chapter 110, "Queequeg in His Coffin"). In adapting religious "theory" to body art first and decorative carving next, Queequeg models the creative migration of text across media. Religion, art, and culture meet in the dynamic designs on Queequeg's body for all to see, though as Ishmael mourns, they "were therefore destined in the end to moulder [*sic*] away with the living parchment whereon they were inscribed, and so be unsolved to the last."

Through these characters Melville represents the imaginative use and reuse, adaptation and dissemination, writing and remediating of a wide range of materials and texts. We might think of Melville's direct borrowings or allusions as exhibiting different attitudes: admiration and respect, mockery and parody, mimicry or even unacknowledged theft, or resistance and challenge. Examples of all of these appear in the opening chapter, "Loomings."

Admiration and Respect

We call this attitude one that declares, "I like it. I'll take it." Melville litters the text with direct references to familiar and favorite works, as noted above. In "Loomings," he borrows a "philosophical flourish" from Cato (describing Ishmael's motives for going to sea); a bit of aesthetic theory from Burke (talking about artists and the picturesque); the myth of Narcissus (to describe the allure of the watery world); stoic philosophy from Seneca; divine judgment from the Bible (in a reference to whether the archangel Gabriel will think less of Ishmael for signing on to a vessel); a theatrical "programme" (listing a "WHALING VOYAGE BY ONE ISHMAEL") and various dramatic forms (tragedies, comedies, farces) to suggest he is but a player in the hands of "those stage managers, the Fates."

Parody

Melville also mocks and makes fun of his sources. During a period in which readers were raptly absorbing the new discoveries in Egyptology, references to the Pyramids seldom appeared as a way to describe broiled chicken, but Melville does so here: "It is out of the idolatrous dotings of the old Egyptians upon broiled ibis and roasted river horse, that you see the mummies of those creatures in their huge bakehouses the pyramids." He jokes about a "Pythagorean maxim" concerning beans and flatulence, using it to claim that sailors have an advantage over their captain, who "gets his atmosphere at second hand from the sailors on the forecastle."

Mimicry

Melville often adopts the voices of different texts or speakers, directly appropriating their typical language. So, for example, he writes in the style of a New York City guidebook: "Circumambulate the city of a dreamy Sabbath afternoon. Go from Corlears Hook to Coenties Slip, and from thence, by Whitehall, northward. What do you see?"; or of an art critic: "Deep into distant woodlands winds a mazy way, reaching to overlapping spurs of mountains bathed in their hill-side blue"; or a sailor: "True, they rather order me about some, and make me jump from spar to spar, like a grasshopper in a May meadow."

Challenge

At times Melville's references imply not respect for the source but a challenge to it. Hence in his allusion to Adam and Eve he serves up a sturdy rebuttal to the doctrine of *felix culpa*, or fortunate fall: "The act of paying is perhaps the most uncomfortable infliction that the two orchard thieves entailed upon us." He speaks irreverently of Providence as a theater "programme" and the Fates as "stage managers" whose machinations "induced me to set about performing the part I did, besides cajoling me into the delusion that it was a choice resulting from my own unbiased freewill and discriminating judgment."

Throughout the novel, Melville makes many more and different kinds of borrowings from different kinds of texts. Is he showing off? To some extent he is. We can ignore them, but even if we pay attention to only a small number, we soon get a sense of his imaginative use of these references, which suggest a rich, ongoing dialogue with authors he loved and admired but also ridiculed and debunked.

MELVILLE AS LENDER

When so many literary materials borrowed from different sources take up space in a text, students may feel crowded out. How do you read a text that is itself full of books? Do you have to be a scholar to enjoy *Moby-Dick*? But authors can also create ways for readers to enter the text imaginatively themselves, to begin telling their own stories in dialogue with the literary tradition the author has evoked. Pointing out to students what the author has left open allows them to intervene in the creative process, much as they do in their own fan practices online. *They* become the borrowers, the classic text a lender of imaginative space.

This notion of what gets left out of a literary work and how readers may step into the breach has not traditionally entered into language arts classes—not mine, anyway. Readers and teachers of literary texts are generally more involved with what an author *does* in writing a text than in what he or she *does not* do. When I teach *Pride and Prejudice*, and students ask, "Why don't they kiss at the end?" the typical response is "Well, now you've stepped outside the book. That's not the book Austen wrote. We're here to talk about the book Austen wrote." Yet numerous films and books have filled in Austen's story, and you can be sure that most of them end with a kiss. These reworkings, while often not "true" to the original work, nevertheless step outside the book boldly and read it in new ways. They are part of the long line of interpretations of the text and as such are relevant in the way scholarly articles or Austen-themed tourist sites or other kinds of interpretation are relevant.

Moby-Dick has inspired probably more spinoffs—illustrated editions, abridgments, films, cartoons, restaurants, television episodes, jokes, comic books, parodies, songs, even a heavy metal album—than any other American novel. This wealth of cultural material suggests a large fan following, certainly, but also the endless adaptability of the book's themes and characters. *Moby-Dick* inspires readers to rewrite it in different media and new idioms and voices, as Ricardo Pitts-Wiley's *Moby-Dick: Then and Now* abundantly reveals.

But how can students begin rewriting a book that seems so large and complete in itself? In fact, *Moby-Dick* leaves many gaps for a reader to fill. This point might draw immediate gasps of disbelief, since the response of many readers, even when it was first published in 1851, has been to criticize the book's length and plenitude. It is *too* long. How can one complain about what has been left out? Nothing has been left out. Everything, as Melville says in his opening "Extracts," "affording a glancing bird's eye view of what has been promiscuously said, thought, fancied, and sung of Leviathan, by many nations and generations, including our own," has been included in the book. If you want to know all there is to know about whaling, and a great deal more besides, read *Moby-Dick*.

Yet especially in the late 20th and early 21st centuries, as literary scholarship has opened up the so-called literary canon to new, previously unheard or unrecognized voices, the question of which readers Melville reached and which he neglected, what characters or groups he represented and which he represented unsatisfactorily or not at all, has become more urgent and critical.

One gap that has in more recent years appeared a glaring one is the absence of women in the book. Yes, certain women appear—Mrs. Hussey at the Try-Pots, Aunt Charity in Nantucket, the Polynesian island women who grace the decks of "a Nantucket ship, the Bachelor" in Chapter 115. Wives of the departing sailors appear as an undifferentiated group in Chapter 7, "The Chapel," listening in "muffled silence" to Father Mapple's sermon. Starbuck mentions his wife, and Ahab has a wife, who has inspired a one-woman theater piece and an art installation, Ellen Driscoll's Ahab's Wife (1997), as well as Sena Jeter Naslund's novel of the same name (1999). Nevertheless no women play active roles in the book, a fact that has concerned critics, readers, and serious adaptors like Ricardo Pitts-Wiley.

In addressing this gender gap readers ask, "Why doesn't Melville include women in his book?" The question is hard to answer satisfactorily and tends to limit one's understanding and exploration of the text. Do we ask why Toni Morrison does not write at great length about White people? Is it a problem that Amy Tan writes her books from a predominantly female and Asian or Asian American point of view? More useful for reading practices in a participatory culture would be the question, What spaces does Melville create in his text for imagining women or people of different races, nationalities, or sexual identities? As seen in the outpouring of multimedia adaptations of *Moby-Dick,* including ones with multiracial, feminist, or gay characters and themes, the book affords many opportunities for readers of different identities and backgrounds to insert themselves into the text.

SPACES AND SILENCES: WHERE CREATIVITY BEGINS

The silence of *Moby-Dick* on the many kinds of people it might have included in the text might seem exclusive and prohibitive. Melville's multicultural chapter, "Midnight, Forecastle," names sailors from the Azores, Africa, China, Tahiti, and many other places that do not tend to get noticed in 19th-century literature except as exotic or abstract locations. But the sailors themselves are almost invisible, not meriting the close attention and character development with which Melville invests his White characters. Even as fully realized a character as Queequeg mostly disappears after the first 23 chapters, to emerge only briefly after that. But Melville's silences speak to another possibility as well. In many of Melville's works silence conveys meaning and power. The whale Moby Dick, who motivates the whole novel and gives it its title, is notably silent throughout. How many eponymous heroes (Jane Eyre, David Copperfield, Jay Gatsby, Rabbit) never utter a word throughout an entire book? The whale's silence nevertheless generates hundreds of thousands of words and allows Ishmael to narrate a massive work. To Melville silence is sublime and majestic. More important for our students, the silences of the text create a space for new understandings of power and new writing and creativity.

For example, silence creates a majestic space around Ahab in Chapter 34, "The Cabin-Table," where he "presided like a mute, maned sea-lion on the white coral beach, surrounded by his warlike but still deferential cubs." So intimidated are the mates that their meals pass "in awful silence." But silence is not reserved only for the White captain. In Chapter 17, "The Ramadan," for example, after investigating the *Pequod* and deciding it is the ship for him, Ishmael returns to the Try-Pots to tell Queequeg the news.

Instead of the friendly reception he has enjoyed so far, however, he meets a locked door, and when he knocks and calls, no answer comes. After various feints and starts, Ishmael breaks down the door to discover Queequeg observing a day-long fast and meditation, his "Ramadan." Ishmael finds Queequeg's silence and discipline so unnerving that he hardly knows what to do or think. Yet although he lectures him afterward about the dangers of long fasts, he is also clearly impressed by Queequeg's religious faith. Furthermore he accepts as fact Queequeg's implication that "he no doubt thought he knew a good deal more about the true religion than I did." In the physical space Queequeg creates between them by locking the door, and in the length of time during which he refuses his companionship, Queequeg creates a powerful place for himself in the text.

In Chapter 93, "The Castaway," Pip too gains power from creating a sphere of silence and, in his case, infinite space around himself. Pip has been ejected from Stubb's whaleboat during a chase and floats alone in the sea for hours before the men find him. During that time he experiences "the intense concentration of self in the middle of such a heartless immensity." In the endless space and silence in which he contemplates the universe, Pip "saw God's foot on the treadle of the loom, and spoke it." Afterward the sailors call him mad, but he also achieves a special status on the ship and eventually moves into Ahab's cabin as his confidant and companion. Pip has hardly spoken before except through his tambourine and the eloquent soliloquy in "Midnight, Forecastle." After the loss of his wits, although he now speaks in gibberish or riddles, his speech has a power that competes with Ahab's.

No being conveys more eloquently the power of silence than Moby Dick himself. In Chapter 52, "The Spirit-Spout," the sailors detect on the horizon a mysterious "silvery jet" that Ishmael is convinced comes from the whale. It appears in the "silvery silence" of a "silent night" always at the "same silent hour." What might seem in another context beautiful looks sinister here, engendering "a sense of peculiar dread, . . . as if it were treacherously beckoning us on and on, in order that the monster might turn round upon us, and rend us at last in the remotest and most savage seas." When Moby Dick does appear in full view at the end of the novel, he once again comes in awesome silence, "at every roll of the sea revealing his high sparkling hump, and regularly jetting his silent spout into the air."

Melville was later to write in his poem "The Great Pyramid" of the power of God as the "dumb I AM." Silent characters appear in nearly all his works—Bartleby, the scrivener, comes most strikingly to mind, but there are many others—each one invested with a remarkable power to strike the reader with awe. The silences in *Moby-Dick*, coming in the midst of Ishmael's wordy narrative, suggest the spaces within the text where unimaginable power may dwell. Frequently this silence is associated with characters like Queequeg, Pip, and Moby Dick, who, in the world of Melville's urban middle-class White readers, would be otherwise powerless and speechless.

The silence, then, of the women in Father Mapple's church or of the "dumb brute" Moby Dick or of Pip, Daggoo, and Tashtego does not necessarily imply that these characters have been marginalized or silenced. Melville reserves for them a space that resonates with meaning—a "negative" space with a positive charge. It is not surprising, then, that numerous readers have felt empowered to take up their own places in Melville's text and begin writing.

"FRIENDS, HOLD MY ARMS!": MELVILLE'S INVITATION TO THE READER

One of the reasons *Moby-Dick* has produced so many adaptations, translations, parodies, and remediations is that Melville models this kind of creative work himself in the way he writes his book. As we have seen, he adapts and rewrites Shakespeare, the Bible, Milton, and Beale with enthusiastic abandon. Some of his borrowings suggest deep reverence for his sources, others a more frivolous desire to adorn his text or to parody and subvert his competitors. In these maneuvers, Melville invites a reader to do likewise, if he or she can, with *Moby-Dick*. In Chapter 104, as often elsewhere in the text, Ishmael speaks directly to his readers: "Give me a condor's quill! Give me Vesuvius's crater for an inkstand! Friends, hold my arms! For in the mere act of penning my thoughts of this Leviathan, they weary me, and make me faint with their outreaching comprehensiveness of sweep." Calling upon his readers as friends, Ishmael implies that they can join him in his weighty enterprise and even write books of their own.

The passage also shows, however, that more than friendship and goodwill is required; one must also exercise judgment. Acknowledging what his readers must already know, Ishmael calls his book a vast enterprise: "To produce a mighty book, you must choose a mighty theme." Ishmael claims to have *chosen* "to include the whole circle of the sciences, and all the generations of whales, and men, and mastodons, past, present, and to come, with all the revolving panoramas of empires on earth, and throughout the whole universe, not excluding its suburbs." This statement speaks to authorial decision-making, about both what to include and what to leave aside. Ishmael does not seem to have forgotten or neglected anything in *Moby-Dick*, but in fact the book is full of roads not taken. As Ishmael models certain kinds of choices, he also indicates things not chosen. In the spaces created by those unchosen possibilities, readers, his friends, may insert narratives of their own.

These roads not taken provide openings for Ishmael's comrades. Just as Melville's fleeting glimpses of women make possible *Ahab's Wife*, so some of the anomalies, absences, silences, and spaces indicated elsewhere in the text could engender *What Bulkington Knew*, *How Ishmael Got Home: An Odyssey*, *Queequeg, Prince of Polynesia*, and *Son of Starbuck*. The spaces in the narrative can be seen not simply as lapses on Melville's part but also as rich possibilities for new stories. Such a perspective enables participation in Melville's world but also, more broadly, in the world generated by his book and by the people who have read and shared it with other friends. The power of the book resides as much in what it does not say or do as in what it tells us on the page.

CHAPTER 12

Reading Critically and Reading Creatively

Henry Jenkins

If there is a shared agenda within the diversity and fragmentation that has often characterized the American media literacy movement, it has come through a focus on five core questions students and teachers have been taught to apply to a range of texts:

- Who created this message?
- What creative techniques are used to attract my attention?
- How might different people understand this message differently from me?
- What lifestyles, values, and points of view are represented in, or omitted from, this message?
- Why is this message being sent? (Center for Media Literacy, n.d.)

The *TSG* addresses each of these core questions, although not always in the same language. When we talk about context in our discussion of remix, we are really trying to consider who created the message and why; we also encourage students to identify the techniques deployed within the remix. Our discussion of motives for reading helps to explain how and why "different people understand this message differently from me," and that recognition of differences in interpretation and experience are central to our understanding of how to negotiate a multicultural space. Throughout, we have reinforced the value of close reading. We have embraced the core goals of the media literacy tradition, but we are also expanding its vocabulary and introducing some new perspectives. We are trying to reflect through our pedagogy some significant shifts in the media environment.

In this chapter, we want to turn our attention to question 4—What lifestyles, values, and points of view are represented in, or omitted from, this message? Here, pay attention to the word *omitted*. What's not in the text is read as consciously or unconsciously excluded; often there's a hint that certain perspectives are being silenced, marginalized, or repressed. This formulation sets the reader in ideological opposition to the text while maintaining a clear separation between producers and consumers. This understanding reflects a moment when the power of mass media was extensive and the average consumer had no real way to respond to the media's agenda except through critical analysis. In a participatory culture, however, any given work represents a provocation for further creative responses. When we read a blog or a post on a forum, when we watch a video on YouTube, the possibility exists for us to respond—either critically or creatively. We can write a fierce rebuttal of an argument with which we disagree or we can create a new work that better reflects our point of view.

Schools have historically taught students how to read with the goal of producing a critical response; we want to encourage educators to also teach students how to engage creatively with texts. Under this model, we should still be concerned with what's not in the text; the difference is in what we do about it. Yochai Benkler (2007) argues that we look at the world differently in a participatory culture; we look at it through the eyes of someone who can participate. Just as we read for different things depending on our goals, we also watch for different things depending on whether we want to use the experience of reading as the starting point for writing criticism or as a springboard for creative expression. At its worst, reading critically teaches us to dismiss texts with which we disagree. At its best, reading creatively empowers us to rewrite texts that don't fully satisfy our interests. Keep in mind that we may rewrite a text out of fascination, out of frustration, or often out of a complex mixture of the two.

READING FAN FICTION

Fan fiction represents a vivid example of reading creatively and critically. *Fan fiction* refers to original stories and novels set in the fictional universes of favorite television series, films, comics, games, or other media properties. Today, fans write thousands of stories each year devoted to hundreds of different media texts. The writers are often amateur; the stories are labors of love. Many of these stories are distributed online. Historically, women wrote the majority of fan stories, though men have become more actively involved as fan fiction has moved onto the web. Fan authors and critics have developed their own vocabulary for talking about these works with many of the terms reflecting fan-oriented genres or describing the complex set of negotiations between the fan text and the source text. Some of the terms reflect the desire of fans to respect the original work, such as the distinction between stories that are "in" or "out" of character; others, such as "alternate universe," signal works that break more dramatically with the original material.

In her book, *The Democratic Art*, poet Sheenagh Pugh (2006) discusses what motivates people to write fan fiction. She suggests that some fans want "more from" the original source material because they felt something was missing, and some write because they want "more of" the original source material, because the story raises expectations that are not fulfilled. Pugh discusses stories as addressing two related questions—"what if" and "what else" (p. 17). Pugh's discussion moves between fans writing about science fiction or cop shows and fans writing about literary classics (for example, Jane Austen's novels). She focuses mostly on the work of amateur writers, yet she also acknowledges that a growing number of professional writers are turning their lenses on canonical literature and extending it in new directions. She opens her book, for example, with a discussion of John Reed's *Snowball's Chance*, which rewrites George Orwell's *Animal Farm*. Other examples might include Isabel Allende's *Zorro* (based on a pulp magazine character), Gregory Maguire's *Wicked* (*The Wizard of Oz*), Jean Rhys's *Wide Sargasso Sea* (*Jane Eyre*), Tom Stoppard's *Rosencrantz and Guildenstern Are Dead* (*Hamlet*), J. M. Coetzee's *Foe* (*Robinson Crusoe*), Linda Berdoll's *Mr. Darcy Takes a Wife* (*Pride and Prejudice*), Nicholas Meyer's *Seven Percent Solution* (Sherlock Holmes), Alice Randall's *The Wind Done Gone* (*Gone with the Wind*), and Sena Jeter Naslund's *Ahab's Wife* (*Moby-Dick*).

While such works are sometimes described as postmodern, such practices run throughout the history of literature and as Abigail Derecho (2006) notes, this mode of creative reworking of canonical literature has been a historical way some female authors have asserted their perspectives in their culture. If anything, modern conceptions of copyright have slowed down a long-standing tendency to retell existing stories. Fan fiction revitalizes that creative impulse, operating in a world where many different people might retell the same story and, in the process, expand the range of potential interpretations of the source material. Here, for example, a veteran fan fiction writer speaks about what motivates her to read and write such stories:

> What I love about fandom is the freedom we have allowed ourselves to create and recreate our characters over and over again. Fanfic rarely sits still. It's like a living, evolving thing, taking on its own life, one story building on another, each writer's reality bouncing off another's and maybe even melding together to form a whole new creation. A lot of people would argue that we're not creative because we build on someone else's universe rather than coming up with our own. However, I find that fandom can be extremely creative because we have the ability to keep changing our characters and giving them new life over and over. We can kill and resurrect them as often as we like. We can change their personalities and how they react to situations. We can take a character and make him charming and sweet or coldblooded and cruel. We can give them an infinite, always-changing life rather than the single life of their original creation. We have given ourselves license to do whatever we want and it's very liberating. . . . If a story moves or amuses us, we share it; if it bothers us, we write a sequel; if it disturbs us, we may even re-write it! We also continually recreate the characters to fit our images of them or to explore a new idea. We have the power and that's a very strong siren. If we want to explore an issue or see a particular scenario, all we have to do is sit down and write it. (Green, Jenkins, & Jenkins, 2006, p. 86)

This statement beautifully captures our participatory model of reading: The text as written is the starting point; readers may be motivated to respond to the work by creating new works. Literary works do not simply enlighten us; they also inspire us or, perhaps more accurately, they provoke us.

Many literary critics would describe a great book as one where everything is there for a reason and nothing is missing. Director's cuts and DVD extras suggest otherwise. At least in the worlds of film and television, many things remain on the cutting room floor; some of what gets left out improves the work by its absence, some of it might have made a meaningful contribution, and some may radically transform our understanding of the whole. DVDs often label these segments "deleted scenes," inviting us to take pleasure in seeing behind the scenes in the production process and second-guessing the producers' creative decisions. For example, the DVD for *Aliens* includes a scene where Ripley reacts to the news that her daughter has grown up and died during the time she has been in suspended animation in space; the scene offers a different understanding of what motivates her intense efforts to protect and rescue the young girl Newt. A scene added for the director's cut of *Blade Runner*, linking Deckard's dream of a unicorn (in the original cut) with a shot of an origami unicorn left outside his dorm (in the director's cut) implies that he may be a replicant, because people from the corporation know the contents of his dreams.

We might contrast this focus on deleted scenes with a genre of fan fiction called "missing scenes." Here, fans add to the fiction, offering their own versions of what might have happened during scenes absent from the original source. These scenes may be as simple as showing how other characters reacted to the news of the events shown in a particular episode; they might show us what happened before or after a key turning point, allowing us a deeper understanding of the character's motivations or the impact of their actions. So, the term *deleted scenes* holds on to the idea that authors get to determine what belongs in their story, while *missing scenes* allows fans to decide for themselves what parts of the story felt absent. Both can represent creative contributions to our understanding of the work but they have different status because our culture tends to value the original author over their readers.

READING *MOBY-DICK* AS A FAN

Fans are searching for unrealized potentials in the story that might provide a springboard for their own creative activities. We might identify at least five basic elements that can inspire fan interventions. Learning to read as a fan often involves learning to find such openings (Bacon-Smith, 1992).

Kernels

> *Kernels*: Pieces of information introduced into a narrative to hint at a larger world but not fully developed within the story itself.

Kernels typically pull us away from the core plot line and introduce other possible stories to explore. For example, consider the meeting between the captains of the *Pequod* and the *Rachel* near the end of Melville's novel (Chapter 128). Captain Gardiner of the *Rachel* is searching for a missing boat, lost the night before, with his own son aboard. He solicits Ahab's help: "For you too have a boy, Captain Ahab—though but a child, and nestling safely at home now—a child of your old age too." The detail is added here to show how much Ahab is turning his back on all that is human in himself. Yet this one phrase contains the seeds of an entire story of how and why Ahab had a son at such a late age, what kind of father Ahab might have been, and so forth. We may also wonder how Gardiner knows about Ahab's son, since the book describes him as a "stranger." The John Huston film version goes so far as to suggest that Gardiner was also from New Bedford, which opens up the possibility that the two men knew each other in the past. What did their previous relationship look like? Were they boyhood friends or bitter rivals? Were their wives sisters? Did the two sons know each other? Might Ahab's wife have babysat for Gardiner's son? Soon, we have the seeds of a new story about these two men and their families.

Holes

> *Holes*: Plot elements readers perceive as missing from the narrative but central to their understanding of its characters.

Holes typically affect the primary plot. For example, consider the story of how Ahab lost his leg. In many ways, this story is central to the trajectory of the novel, but we receive only fragmentary bits of information about what actually happened and why this event has had such a transformative impact on Ahab, while other seamen we meet have adjusted more fully to the losses of life and limb that are to be expected in pursuing such a dangerous profession. What assumptions do readers make about who Ahab was—already a captain, a young crew member on board someone else's ship—or where he was when this incident occurred? In fandom, a large number of different stories might explain what happened; each version might reflect a different interpretation of Ahab's character.

Contradictions

> *Contradictions*: Two or more elements in the narrative (intentionally or unintentionally) suggesting alternative possibilities for the characters.

Are the characters in *Moby-Dick* doomed from the start, as might be suggested by the prophecies of Elijah and Gabriel? Does this fact suggest some model of fate or divine retribution, as might be implied by Father Mapple's sermon? Or might we see the characters as exerting a greater control over what happens to them, having the chance to alter the course of events, as is implied by some of the exchanges between Ahab and Starbuck? Different writers could construct different stories depending on how they think about the nature of free will. And we can imagine several stories emerging around the mysterious figure of Elijah. Is Elijah someone gifted with extraordinary visions? Is he a madman? Does he have a history with Ahab that might allow him insights into the captain's character and thus allow Elijah to anticipate his likely choices?

Silences

> *Silences*: Elements that were systematically excluded from the narrative with ideological consequences.

As Wyn Kelley notes, many writers have complained about the absence of female characters in *Moby-Dick*, suggesting that we cannot fully understand the world of men without also understanding the experience of women. Some works—such as the John Huston version—call attention to the place of women in whaling culture, if only incidentally. Melville hints at this culture only through a few scattered references to the families Ahab and Starbuck left behind. These references can provide the starting point for a different story, as occurs in Sena Jeter Naslund's novel *Ahab's Wife*; we might imagine another version of the story where Ahab was female, as occurs in *Moby-Dick: Then and Now*, or we might use the plot of *Moby-Dick* as the starting point for creating a totally different story set in another kind of world where women can play the same kind of roles as the men play in Melville's novel, as occurs in the *Battlestar Galactica* episode "Scar."

Potentials

> *Potentials*: Projections about what might have happened beyond the borders of the narrative.

Many readers finish a novel and find themselves wanting to speculate about "what happens next." As Pugh writes, "Whenever a canon closes, someone somewhere will mourn it enough to reopen it. . . . Even though we may feel that the canonical ending is 'right' artistically, if we liked the story we may still not be ready for it to end, for the characters and milieu that have become real to us to be folded up and put back in the puppeteer's box" (2006, p. 17). For example, we might wonder what kind of person Ishmael becomes after being rescued. Melville offers us some hints—even if only because Ishmael chooses to tell this story in the first place. Yet in our world, someone like Ishmael might be wracked with "survivor guilt," feeling responsibility for the deaths of his friends, or wondering why he alone made it through alive. How might Ishmael have dealt with these powerful emotions? How might these events have changed him from the character we see at the start of the novel? Might we imagine some future romance that "comforts" him through his "hurts"?

The examples above suggest several additional aspects of reading a narrative as a fan. First, fans generally focus on characters and their relationships as their point of entry. Melville's novel, with its digressions and fragmentation, raises many more character issues than it resolves—for example, the richly drawn but only occasionally explored friendship between Ishmael and Queequeg, or for that matter, the comradeship between Queequeg, Daggoo, and Tashtego, or the relationship between Ahab and Fedallah. Second, fans look for worlds that are richer, have greater potentials, than can be "used up" within a single story. They are particularly interested in backstory—the untold narratives that explain how the characters became the people we encounter. Many contemporary television series reward this fan interest by parceling out bits and fragments of backstory. Part of the pleasure of reading *Moby-Dick* is absorbing all the incidental details about the ship, its crew, the other ships, and life in New Bedford; and through chapters such as "The Town-Ho's Story," Melville tells us that this world is full of stories beyond the ones the novel tells.

For the most part, fan reading practices are directed at popular television series or films, but there's no reason why they can't be applied to works from the literary canon. Teachers might find that many students respond well to being asked to look at *Moby-Dick* and other literary texts through this lens.

Here's a process you might follow:

- Encourage students to find examples of kernels, holes, contradictions, silences, and potentials.
- Ask them to consider what purposes these elements play within the original novel.

- Invite them to speculate on how these elements might provide the basis for additional stories.
- Tell them to find other passages that provide insight into the core character relationships here.
- Discuss what elements would need to be in place for a new story to feel that it belongs in this fictional world.
- Have students write stories reflecting their insights.
- Share stories between students, especially those working with the same elements, so that they have a sense of the very different ways writers might build upon these same starting points.

Ricardo Pitts-Wiley took a very similar approach with the students in the Rhode Island correctional program, asking them to select a character and explore the novel from their point of view. Students were encouraged to develop a character sketch that described what kind of person the character would be if he or she were alive today. These character sketches were then combined to construct a plot in which these characters met at the Spouter Inn and set out on a quest together. Such an approach might tap the techniques of fantasy role-play games to sketch out the events of the story, and then the student writers might contribute to a shared narrative of the experience.

THE "TRANSFORMATIVE WORK" OF FAN CULTURE

Fan stories are not simply "extensions" or "continuations" of the original series. They are constructing arguments through new stories rather than critical essays. Although a literary essay generally responds to its subject in nonfictional form, fan fiction uses fiction to respond to fiction. You will find all kinds of argumentation about interpretation woven through most fan-produced stories. A good fan story references key events or bits of dialogue as evidence to support its particular interpretation of the characters' motives and actions. Secondary details are deployed to suggest that the story might have plausibly occurred in the fictional world depicted in the original. There are certainly bad stories that don't dig deeply into the characters or fall back on fairly banal interpretations, but good fan fiction displays a deep respect for the source material and explores some aspect that has sparked the fan writer's imagination or curiosity. Fan fiction is speculative, but it is also interpretative. And more than this, it is creative.

The fan writer wants to create a new story that is entertaining in its own right and offer it to perhaps the most demanding audience you could imagine—other deeply invested experts about the original work.

Novelist Michael Chabon has written an essay discussing the value of fan fiction in relation to Sherlock Holmes:

> All enduring popular literature has this open-ended quality, and extends this invitation to the reader to continue, on his or her own, with the adventure. . . . It creates a sense of an infinite horizon of play, an endless game board; it spawns, without trying, a thousand sequels, diagrams, and web sites. . . . Through parody and pastiche, allusion and homage, retelling and reimagining the stories that were told before us and that we have come of age loving—amateurs—we proceed, seeking out the blank places in the map that our favorite writers, in their greatness and negligence, have left for us, hoping to pass on to our own readers—should we be lucky enough to find any—some of the pleasure that we ourselves have taken in the stuff we love: to get in on the game. All novels are sequels; influence is bliss. (2008, p. 44)

Not all writers would agree that writing fan fiction is a logical or legitimate extension of critical interpretation. Fantasy writer Robin Hobb has raised sharp concerns about how fan fiction impacts her own creative process:

> Every fan fiction I've read to date, based on my world or any other writer's world, has focused on changing the writer's careful work to suit the foible of the fan writer. Romances are invented, gender identities changed, fetishes indulged and endings are altered. It's not flattery. To me, it is the fan fiction writer saying, "Look, the original author really screwed up the story, so I'm going to fix it. Here is how it should have gone." . . . A writer puts a great deal of thought into what goes into the story and what doesn't. If a particular scene doesn't happen "on stage" before the reader's eyes, there is probably a reason for it. If something is left nebulous, it is because the author intends for it to be nebulous. . . . Fan fiction closes up the space that I have engineered into the story, and the reader is told what he must think rather than being allowed to observe the characters and draw his own conclusions. (quoted in Justin, 2005)

By contrast, consider this statement from the introduction to an important anthology of scholarly essays about fan fiction:

> Work in progress is a term used in the fan fiction world to describe a piece of fiction still in the process of being written but not yet completed. . . . The appeal of works in progress lies in part in the ways fans engage with an open text; it invites responses, permits shared authorship, and enjoins a sense of community. . . . Every fan story is in this sense a work in progress, even when the story has been completed. . . . In most cases, the resulting story is part collaboration and part response to not only the source text, but also the cultural context within and outside the fannish community in which it is produced. (Busse & Hellekson, 2006, p. 6)

These writers see both the fan text and the source text as open-ended, subject to revision and expansion, providing raw material for further speculation and creative elaboration. This idea of the text as open and collaborative contrasts sharply with Hobb's notion that writers should have the last word and that any addition by fans is to be understood as signaling a flaw or error. Fans would find Hobb's suggestion that their stories tell the reader "what he must think rather than being allowed to observe the characters and draw his own conclusions" particularly baffling, since no fan story is regarded as in any way definitive or as precluding other acts of authorship. To the contrary, fans take great pleasure in reading and writing different interpretations of the shared characters, and fan authors often may construct a number of mutually contradictory conceptions of the characters or situations even within their own body of work.

Some fans have adopted the legal term *transformative works* to defend their creative practices against such challenges. A transformative use is one that, in the words of the U.S. Supreme Court, "adds something new, with a further purpose or different character, altering the [source] with new expression, meaning, or message." *Moby-Dick: Then And Now* is a transformative work insofar as it revises and updates Melville's novel. *Moby-Dick* is a transformative work insofar as it takes sources, such as the story of "Jonah," as raw materials for its own storytelling. And fan fiction is transformative insofar as it transforms the critical insights we are discussing here into the starting point for new stories, developing new conceptualizations of the characters or expanding the narrative in new directions.

SHOULD FANS BE SCHOOLED?

There has also emerged a strong set of arguments about the educational benefits of the fan community as a space of informal learning, especially for younger fans. More and more literacy experts are recognizing that enacting, reciting, and appropriating elements from pre-existing stories is a valuable and organic part of the process by which children develop cultural literacy. Educators like to talk about "scaffolding," the ways that a good pedagogical process works in a step-by-step fashion, encouraging kids to try out new skills that build on those they have already mastered, providing support for these new steps until the learner feels sufficient confidence to take them on his or her own. In the classroom, the teacher provides this scaffolding. In a participatory culture, the entire community takes on some responsibility for helping newbies find their way. Many young writers began composing stories as a spontaneous response to popular culture. For these young writers, the next step was the discovery of fan fiction on the Internet, which provided alternative models for what it meant to be an author. At first, they might only read stories, but the fan community provides many incitements for readers to cross that last threshold into composing and submitting their stories. And once a fan submits, feedback inspires further and improved writing.

Many fan fiction websites provide a process of mentoring, known as "beta-reading," through which more experienced writers critique and support emerging contributors. Fans learn both from the feedback they receive and from the process of sharing feedback with others. As a consequence, fans become better readers and writers. As educational researcher Rebecca Black (2008) argues, the fan community can often be more tolerant of linguistic errors than are traditional classroom teachers and more helpful in enabling learners to identify what they are actually trying to say because reader and writer operate within the same frame of reference, sharing a deep emotional investment in the content being explored. The fan community promotes a broader range of different literary forms—not simply fan fiction but various modes of commentary—than the exemplars available to students in the classroom, and often they showcase realistic next steps for the learner's development rather than showing only professional writing that is far removed from anything most students will be able to produce.

Much of what works here works because fan fiction exists outside school, and the people who participate do so out of deep personal and social motivations, rather than because they are assigned to write a story for a grade. Yet this does not mean that educators cannot learn a good deal from fan fiction. We believe strongly that there is value in learning to engage with works of fiction creatively as well as critically, that the process of creating a transformative work often motivates a much closer reading of the original text, that it is empowering for young people to think of themselves as authors and thus to find their own expressive voices, especially in the context of today's participatory culture.

Part IV

BEYOND *MOBY-DICK*: CHALLENGES AND OPPORTUNITIES

CHAPTER 13

Reading and Negotiation

Hillary Kolos and
Judith Nierenberg

This is not your typical classroom. Mannequin heads line one wall, their hair braided or feathered. A poster hangs above the whiteboard detailing a hair follicle. The bookshelf holds a rainbow of nail polish bottles. Fifteen cosmetology students are deep in conversation about the meaning of culture. The discussion so far has been about cultures foreign to the students, but a young woman with dark brown hair brings the conversation closer to home: "Culture is something you carry inside of you. It comes from the people around you." This simple but powerful definition strikes to the core of what this class is about.

We sit at the front of the class listening intently to the insights the students offer. Judi is the school librarian, and Hillary is a research assistant from New Media Literacies (NML). We had been working together for several months on a teaching collaboration in the vocational education section of Somerville High School in Somerville, Massachusetts. Judi was invited by cosmetology teachers Stella Apostolakos and Gregory Wright to add a literature component to their class as part of the school's attempt to bridge the academic and vocational sides of the school. We decided to adapt NML's *Teachers' Strategy Guide: Reading in a Participatory Culture* (*TSG*), to be used with a book Judi knew the students would relate to: *Twists and Turns* (McDonald, 2003), a young adult novel that follows two young women who open a hair-braiding salon. The women live in public housing with their mother and enlist their community to help open their business. The book includes instances of culture clash and community activism as outside developers eye the housing projects for high-end condos and local "haters" try to destroy the girls' business.

One of our goals was to explore the new media literacy skill of negotiation: the ability to travel across diverse communities, discerning and respecting multiple perspectives, and grasping and following alternative norms (Jenkins et al., 2009). The students we were working with were in some ways already expert negotiators of culture, whether in fitting in with different peer groups at school or in knowing how to act in class versus how to act at the pizza place after school. Through this class, we hoped to make the students more aware of this skill they already practiced daily and apply it to new contexts, including reading. We recognized that, for students who don't identify as "readers," it can sometimes be difficult to enter a text. In order to make them feel more comfortable as readers, we hoped to help them identify other parts of their lives where they negotiated new cultures so that they could use those skills to negotiate the new cultures they encountered in books.

We use negotiation not only in our face-to-face and online relations with other people, but also internally as we try to define who we are. NML director Henry Jenkins (2009) has said we are moving "towards multiculturalism as part of each individual's construction of identity; rather than negotiating between groups, we are increasingly negotiating amongst competing, sometimes conflicting identities within ourselves." Jenkins's way of thinking about culture and identity is exemplified by the definition the student gave at the beginning of the class.

In the first class, Judi laid out nearly two dozen items she reads each day in addition to books to model the many ways that we are readers. The students then completed a Reading Identity Map that visualized the various reading identities they took on and listed what they read under each one. Their reading identities varied from student to mother to churchgoer to music fan. One young woman realized that she read all the time, whether it was baby formula labels, MySpace pages, textbooks, or her work schedule. Each day, she negotiated between several reading identities.

The purpose of the Reading Identity Map was to prep the students for reading *Twists and Turns*. Before we handed out copies of the book, which they were able to keep, we didn't realize how much it would mean to some of the students. A few remarked they had never owned a book, and one student said she had never read a book. Many were English as a Second Language students with complicated lives that presented obstacles to reading at home, but creating a Reading Identity Map helped them see that reading was an activity in which they already participated.

We spent the next several classes discussing the book and mapping the many characters and their complex relationships. After the students had a handle on who was interacting in the book, we discussed how the characters used negotiation. From the beginning of class, we made a point of relating the book to the students' lives by asking them to talk about what they knew about the issues in the book, such as renting versus owning a home or being "hated on" by others. We attempted to make the boundaries between nonschool and school more porous, allowing students to employ their many skills and experiences and learn from each other. Students easily related to the events of the book and they were eager to volunteer comparable experiences from their own lives.

Our first classes helped prepare us for the complex conversation about culture that opened this chapter. There are several scenes in the book where people of different races, classes, or educational levels interact with each other. Judi started one class with a loaded question: What is culture? At first, the students focused on cultures that were not their own. Once the other students heard the idea that culture is something we carry inside of us, though, they began to share examples from their own lives. Many of the students were born in other countries but had lived in the United States for several years. There was a constant tension in their comments about whether they identified as being from their home country or as being American.

We asked them to explore how they negotiated different cultures. One student brought up the difference between appropriate beachwear in Brazil versus in the United States. We asked how they decided what was appropriate to wear. One student answered that when she went to the beach with her friends she wore a bikini, but with her mom she wore a one-piece. Judi then asked if they had situations at school where they had to make similar decisions about how to present themselves. A round of "Oh, yeahs" rang throughout the room, sparking an animated discussion of the subcultures at the school and what markers identify each group.

To build on this rich conversation, in the next class we introduced an activity from the *TSG* in which students were asked to map the subcultures of their school cafeteria. The class was split into groups by their lunch period and asked to draw a map of where different groups of students sat and how they defined themselves with markers such as what they wore or the music they listened to. The students were eager to work together on the subculture map and were easily able to identify the different groups. Some talked about how they navigated different groups at lunchtime depending on how they were feeling that day—changing their behavior or what they talked about to fit in.

While this activity helped the students see that they were practicing negotiation every day, it also brought up some examples of how students weren't yet experts in the "respecting multiple perspectives" part of how NML defines the skill. For the second part of the activity, the class was asked to annotate another group's cafeteria map to see where they agreed and disagreed with the other group's perspective. When one group of students saw that their friends had been labeled "loud" they were offended, and the comments became more pejorative and led to grouping people by stereotypes. We tried to facilitate the students' comments to be more respectful, but it was clear that this activity was highlighting how the challenge of understanding negotiation goes beyond just recognizing and adapting to other cultures, but also respecting them.

The class continued for a few more sessions, and it ended on a positive note with an activity in which the students each made a mask for a character from *Twists and Turns* and took on the character's role for a conversation about the story. We felt that at the end of the class the students had interacted deeply with the text and related the story to their own experiences successfully. There were some moments that we would do differently, but it did confirm that the general approach and some activities from the *TSG* could be adapted for a book other than *Moby-Dick*.

Judi found the collaboration validated many practices she has employed throughout her years of teaching in museums, schools, and colleges. The process provided her with a new vernacular to describe the methods she has found most successful in helping students become engaged readers. During the school year following the original *TSG* trials, Judi returned to the cosmetology classes with another book, Deborah Rodriguez's *Kabul Beauty School* (2007). The book is the first-person account of Rodriguez's experiences as a beautician in post-Taliban Afghanistan. Beauty shops to prepare brides have always been one of the few avenues for women to work independently in Afghanistan.

The book provides endless examples of cultural negotiation; both Rodriguez and the reader must confront his or her own need to negotiate different cultures. For example, Rodriguez struggles to teach color theory to her students and must turn to using an example of good confronting evil to explain chemical reaction. While many of the students at Somerville High School come from a rich milieu of cultural backgrounds and family lifestyles, several of the students found Rodriguez's marriage to an Afghani man with another wife objectionable. Judi and the students discussed Rodriguez's arrangement with her husband, but for most of the students, it was "not for me." They held fast to the formula of a one-on-one commitment.

This second experience with cosmetology students provided Judi with the opportunity to test her own newly labeled approach to teaching. Rather than the traditional didactic approach of loading students down with maps and journal articles about Afghanistan, the group started by brainstorming what they knew about Afghanistan. Attempting to create a pool of shared information brought out students' reactions to what they had heard or read about cultural differences, as well as personal stories like one about a student's father, who had just completed a tour of duty in Afghanistan with the U.S. Army.

The students in both these classes were already using negotiation in their lives, but we wanted them to be aware of how they did it and how it applied to other aspects of their lives, especially reading. We believe that if the students are able to recognize that they take on various identities, they might become more open to negotiating the new cultural spaces presented to them while reading books.

CHAPTER 14

Lessons from a Classroom Participatory Culture

Jenna McWilliams

The economic crisis over the past half decade has not been kind to the United States' public schools. Much of the country knows this as an abstract fact, as a news item in the local paper announcing the shuttering of some afterschool program or other, or even sometimes announcing the closure of an entire school. For those working in education, however, this fact feels far more concrete; it is evident in the increase in class sizes, in limitations on copying and printing privileges, and in the pink slips handed out to the newest teachers.

For me, the abstract fact became a concrete reality in February 2010, when the school in which I was conducting research, Aurora Alternative High School in Bloomington, Indiana, was closed as part of a sweeping set of cuts, reductions, and closures intended to reduce the district's annual budget by $4.5 million. The proposed cuts were dramatic: All elementary and middle school librarians would be laid off. Middle school foreign language programs would be discontinued. A music instruction program for elementary school students would be shuttered. A popular experiential outdoor education program would be defunded. Most of the safety net programs for struggling students were on the chopping block. The proposal included ending the district's alternative suspension programs, closing down an alternative education program for students who have been expelled or removed from mainstream schooling programs—and shutting down Aurora Alternative High School.

The decision to close the school came after a brief public comment period during which members of the Aurora community—students, parents, and teachers—came together to fight for their school's survival. What emerged at Aurora in the final months of its existence was nothing short of a *participatory culture*: a culture in which all members—teachers, administrators, parents, and students—felt that they *could* contribute and one in which many members *did* contribute to efforts to keep the school open and to support each other when it became clear that the school would be closed. Importantly, although the effort to save the school failed in the short term, their ability to mobilize around a shared concern led to longer-term and lasting changes in the school culture and in the community. In fighting to save their school, students deployed the sorts of core literacy practices that we've tried to foster with our *Teachers' Strategy Guide*. In particular, the practices of negotiation and collective intelligence closely associated with new media literacies became crucial to the students' developing identities as civically engaged youth and, eventually, as youth who would be displaced.

NEGOTIATION

When the school board opened its public comment period in advance of a final vote on its proposed budget cuts, hundreds of community members spoke up in support of the programs they wanted saved. The first public hearing lasted for 4 hours. Dozens of school librarians came out to explain why it was a bad idea to get rid of them. Students and parents spoke in favor of the programs that they felt had saved them or someone they loved. And in the front left corner of the high school auditorium sat dozens of Aurora students, accompanied by parents and teachers, patiently waiting for their turn to speak.

On this evening, the voices speaking in support of Aurora far outnumbered those supporting any other program. Students had written and practiced their own speeches, which they delivered eloquently and with deep maturity. Several audience members, who had come to the meeting to speak in favor of their favorite program, were so swayed by Aurora's students that they changed their minds and spoke in support of Aurora instead. *Before tonight*, one audience member explained, "I didn't even know that Aurora existed. But now I'm convinced that it's the most important program to save."

Linguist and educational researcher James Paul Gee (1992) writes about the big D "Discourse" of public schooling. When given a capital *D*, *Discourse* means the beliefs, values, and ways of thinking and speaking that characterize a community; success in any given community is largely dependent on an individual's ability to master its Discourse. While the Discourse of formal schooling is fairly well aligned with the home discourses of middle- and upper-class kids, working-class kids are at a disadvantage: Their home discourse is not aligned to the Discourse of schools. This means that working-class kids who want to achieve academic success will need to learn to "code switch," to cross communities and alter speech, behavior, style of dress, and so on. In other words, working-class kids who want to achieve academic success will need to master the new media literacies practices of *negotiation*.

As Jenkins et al. (2009) point out, negotiation is an increasingly important practice to master. Today's children are far more likely than ever to encounter a range of communities whose values, beliefs, and ways of thinking, acting, and speaking are unfamiliar. The need for negotiation is even greater for many of Aurora's students, whose schooling experience was often marked by a sense of not fitting in, of not belonging, and even of not knowing how to begin trying to belong.

Aurora was described as the school for students who hadn't experienced success, for whatever reason, in the mainstream public schools in the area. In theory, this meant Aurora could serve students from a range of academic abilities, personal backgrounds, and experiences; in practice, this meant that most—though not all—of Aurora's student body was composed of kids from the most marginalized social groups. The typical Aurora student came to the school after struggling either academically or socially, and sometimes both. Students who were expelled for fighting or other disruptive behavior ended up at Aurora. Students who weren't able to keep up academically with their peers ended up at Aurora. Students who were dealing with pregnancies; homeless kids; kids with arrest records; kids in foster care; kids living on their own; kids whose personalities, values, and interests didn't align with the mainstream all ended up at Aurora. Many Aurora students came from broken homes; some were in foster care; some were in the care of a relative or the parent of a friend; and some lived in a shelter or on their own, as emancipated minors. There was a history of drug use, of fighting, of teen pregnancy among these students. Some had arrest records.

Aurora was filled with tough kids, tougher kids than I'd met anywhere else in the district. Yet when these kids were presented with the prospect of returning to the schools they'd left, these tough kids expressed unease, anxiety, fear. Below, one student, Chris, discusses his future at Central, the school he anticipates moving to if Aurora is closed:

Chris: I'm gonna be scared at Central.

Jason: I don't know if you'll survive.

Stephanie: You won't.

Jason: Like I couldn't survive there my first year. It sucked. It's fucking hell.

(Students' names, and the name of all schools other than Aurora, were changed to protect student privacy.)

Early on in my time at Aurora, Becky Rupert showed me a book of stories students had written about their experiences in the mainstream public school system. In these stories, the *best* experiences were of being almost totally ignored; most described feeling bullied, harassed, and ridiculed. These tough, scared kids were also kids who had been victimized by a system that often didn't like and didn't care about them. They suffered in silence, or they fought back, some of them turning into "problem kids" themselves.

Aurora, in contrast, was a school that cared. No student was ignored; bullying was not tolerated; and all students were given ample opportunity to speak to the rest of the community if they had something to say.

An important part of the Aurora approach to education involved helping kids make decisions about how to navigate community norms. In Becky's classroom, assigned reading helped kids learn about often unfamiliar beliefs and value systems. For several years, Becky had completed a Veterans' History unit that focused on helping kids develop empathy for war veterans. Becky began the unit with Tim O'Brien's *The Things They Carried* (1990), pairing this brutal depiction of the Vietnam conflict with discussion questions and assignments designed to help kids put themselves in the shoes of American soldiers. One activity had kids taking the perspective of a lieutenant who feels responsible for the death of one of his soldiers; students wrote letters to the dead soldier's father from the perspective of this guilty lieutenant. At the end of this unit, students conducted interviews with real-life war veterans. They spent multiple class periods developing a set of questions that would ask the sorts of questions they thought veterans would want to hear.

"*Negotiation*: the ability to travel across diverse communities, discerning and respecting multiple perspectives, and grasping and following alternative norms" (Jenkins et al., 2009, p. xiv).

Early in the *Moby-Dick* unit, Becky used the social networking tool Ning.com to introduce a set of digital tools into class activities. Initial efforts to use these tools for class activities did not go well. When she had students use the chat feature to discuss class readings, they quickly learned how to silence her by sending up a rapid-fire set of nonsense sentences so quickly that she was not able to post her own messages. On members' Facebook-like homepages, students often used offensive language (including racial slurs and sexist expressions) and posted photos that were inappropriate for a school context.

Here was an example of kids assuming that the norms that characterize their youth-only, nonschool online social networks also applied to social networks used for school purposes. There was, however, a new invisible audience (boyd, 2009) in these social networks: teachers, administrators (the school's principal, Chuck Holloway, was among the members of the site), and university researchers.

To help students start to grasp the notion of invisible audiences, Becky had students take a look at comments posted to the online version of the local newspaper, the Bloomington *Herald-Times*. In particular, students looked at comments posted about Aurora. Each year, in response to a news piece announcing Aurora's graduating class, readers made their opinions about the school clear.

"It's almost like graduating from a real school!" exclaimed one reader in response to the paper's 2009 graduation announcement. In 2008, a reader explained that Aurora "is nothing more than a place for social rejects." This reader added a critique of the school's very existence:

> It's not right to give them an alternative. Kids who go to the regular schools choose to try and make it work there. Quit giving kids alternatives. One school. One curriculum. You learn it or you lose. If they don't feel like they fit in, take the individuality away and make them all wear uniforms. The kids who don't like it will probably end up wearing a uniform after school anyway. Likely at a resturant (*sic*), or jail.
> What a bunch of whiney chickenturds.

Becky used students' outrage at these and other comments to guide a conversation about context and unintended audience. They practiced revising their posts to make material appropriate for the context and readership of this online network. This revision did not require that they edited their spelling and grammar, only that they considered whether posted content was appropriate for this context. Becky's efforts in this area were successful enough that later in the semester, when a group of students from another school joined the network and several of these students posted sexually explicit comments, some of Becky's students brought them to her attention.

When students decided to fight to save their school, *negotiation* became a central feature in their efforts. One of their first opportunities to speak on this matter was in a public comment session in which audience members were allotted 3 minutes to speak to the school board and the audience. In preparation for this event, students practiced the "3-minute speech" and spent time considering the rhetorical approach that would most likely be effective for the target audience. Their eloquence and maturity were so compelling that Victoria Ison, a junior at another high school in the district and a student columnist for the *Herald-Times*, posted an open letter to the Aurora community in which she wrote about seeing Aurora's students at the public comment hearing:

> I was surprised to see you there. I was surprised by some of your hats, your earrings, your fashion statements. I was most surprised to see your tears.
>
> Some of you got up and spoke. Eloquently. Emotionally. It was so evident that you were fighting for something you believed in, something you needed.
>
> You talked about being "broken," about being hurt. You talked about needing an escape, wanting to run away. You talked about having to attend any other high school—including my very own North—with measures of overwhelming dread. . . .
>
> Before you spoke, I didn't realize that high school could be such a terrible kind of place. I didn't realize that teenagers—people my own age—could feel hopeless like you said you did. I am sorry for anything I've done to make North such a hard place to be. (2010)

The eloquence of Aurora's student speakers at this public comment hearing was only the beginning. Students sent emails to local school board members and local and state representatives, learning in the process about the norms of formal letter writing. Students also organized public rallies and petition drives in support of their school; in the pit of an Indiana winter, they stood for hours with their signs and their petition sheets. There is an art to approaching complete strangers to request a signature, and Aurora's students learned this art well. As I was walking with friends through the center of town one day, a small cluster of cheerful, red-nosed Aurora kids advanced with clipboards and pens.

"Will you sign our petition to keep Aurora Alternative High School open?" asked Tina, a student I knew from my observations at the school. In school, I had experienced her as a restless young woman who was prone to disruptive behavior; on this sunny and cold February afternoon, however, she was pleasant, polite, knowledgeable, and eager to answer my friends' questions.

The Discourse of the public school system is a foreign one to many of Aurora's students; this is one of the most significant reasons why they have experienced school as a cold, uncaring, alienating place. At Aurora, for the first time, many of these young people not only felt welcomed into the value system of our educational institution but also began to develop strategies for moving between their home discourses and those that characterize many of the institutions of power: education, government, public engagement. Negotiation, for as much as it is a new media literacies skill, is also one that can shift the locus of power, can give the disempowered an opportunity to stand up, with confidence, in front of a community of strangers, and ask for the change they want to see.

COLLECTIVE INTELLIGENCE

One thing that set Aurora apart from other public schools was a fluid hierarchy that placed control and authority not only with teachers and administrators but also with students themselves. This fluidity resulted in large part from the school's emphasis on *collective intelligence*—the ability to pool knowledge and compare notes with others toward a common goal. The "common goal" was an effort to build and support a community of acceptance and mutual respect; and student knowledge was an essential element of making this happen.

Although there was no doubt that, at Aurora, the adults were authority figures who merited respect, students participated in deliberations and decision-making in areas of the most significance to the community. In order to join the community, prospective students were required to submit an application and state their case to an admissions committee made up of teachers and students. Students who had been accepted to the school were expected to abide by the school's rules; when a student was in violation of these rules a committee made up of teachers and students convened to decide how to discipline the student and decide whether the student would be permitted to remain at the school.

Aurora's students were integral in the day-to-day operations of the school, as well. In Becky's class, as in others, attendance taking was a checking-in ritual; if a student was absent, other students generally knew why. Carrie had to stay home to take care of her sick baby. John's car broke down on the way to school. Nobody had heard from Will in a while, but someone heard he might have moved with his dad to Illinois. There wasn't much a group of students could do to help Carrie or Will, but one day as I was walking into the school I heard a young man lean in to Chuck's office and tell him that he had called his older brother and asked him to pick John up and bring him in to school.

The very definition of collective intelligence points at the importance of a shared goal. The Aurora community shared a very clear goal: the establishment and support of a community in which every individual was valued and respected, in which every individual had a right to learn. This goal meant that in the weeks of the brief campaign to save Aurora, students coordinated rides to public hearings, met to draw signs and practice speeches, and checked in with and supported each other when the fear of losing Aurora became intermittently overwhelming.

The campaign to save Aurora was, as I noted above, short-lived. Aurora's students were not the only community members to speak out; educators, parents, students, and community members made their opinions heard to stakeholders across the district. Yet in the end, the school board passed—with a unanimous vote—a final set of cuts that was nearly identical to the set it had proposed. Despite the community's efforts, it appeared, board members had made up their mind to close Aurora before the first student had even spoken.

Students were devastated. A small number would be graduating at the end of the year; most of the rest would choose to transfer back to the high school that had left them feeling marginalized and isolated, or to join a remedial computer-based program, or to simply drop out of school altogether. Yet even as morale dropped and the community prepared to disperse, I watched as Aurora's students made use of networked technologies—primarily mobile phones and Facebook—to continue to extend the emotional support and caring they had received at Aurora.

The Aurora community dissolved at the end of the 2009–2010 school year, but its members remained in contact despite their physical dispersion. Teachers who were laid off or who were placed in another school in the district continued to support each other, in person and through social networks such as Facebook, through the difficult process of integrating into a new school; students used the same resources to stay in contact with each other and with their teachers. Some students reached out for support for their academic aspirations, but others simply kept their former classmates and adult mentors posted on their personal experiences in school and out of it.

For many students, Aurora was the first place where anybody took an interest in their academic future; this was the most difficult thing for some of them to face losing. Students were connected via Facebook with many of their teachers and with the school's principal, Chuck Holloway. After the school was closed and the community had dispersed, former students updated their former teachers and principal on their academic goals and achievements. The teachers, in turn, responded with encouragement and support—the kind that students had lost when they lost their school.

This effort to share information and provide mutual support despite the Aurora community's physical dispersion—this effort to make use of collective intelligence to deal with the devastating loss of a supportive educational community—made it possible for many of these members to reassemble themselves when, in 2011, the district opened a new alternative school program designed to support a group of at-risk students similar to those targeted by Aurora. It cannot be said with certainty that this decision was a result of the increased visibility Aurora's students brought to the district's alternative education programs, but their eloquence, maturity, and determination opened many residents' eyes to the needs of and challenges facing alternative school students.

This new school, called the Bloomington Graduation School, features most of Aurora's staff and several members of Aurora's student body. This school is not Aurora and does not have Aurora's feel—starting a new school is, as anyone who's done it knows, a challenging task—but it was started in the spirit of Aurora, in the spirit of building a community of mutual support and caring, one in which every individual has a right to learn and a motivation to do so.

In defining *participatory culture*, Jenkins et al. (2009) describe it as a culture in which "not all members must contribute, but all must feel free to contribute when ready and that what they contribute will be appropriately valued" (p. 6). This is precisely the culture that emerged in the final months of Aurora's existence: a culture in which members felt empowered to speak, empowered to fight for their community. It wouldn't be precisely fair or accurate to say that Aurora's students got "lucky" in being faced with the loss of their community, but their response to this crisis, and the teachers' role in supporting the students' response, led to the sort of shift that this book strives for: a shift from a system in which students are passive learners and recipients of others' expert knowledge to one in which students are active in constructing knowledge and expertise and in leveraging school to meet their needs and interests.

I was recently talking with a friend, a longtime resident of Bloomington, Indiana, about my struggle to write this chapter. I told her, in vague terms, that I was writing about a time when we told students they had a right to stand up for what they believed in, a time when we told kids they could make a difference—and we were wrong. "What school are you writing about?" she asked. I told her it was an alternative school that she had probably not heard of, that the school was called Aurora, that it was shut down 2 years ago—"

"Oh, right, Aurora!" she interrupted. "I worked with a lot of those kids on public service projects." She paused for a minute.

"You know, you shouldn't feel so bummed about how that went down," she said. "I know you feel like you let the kids down, but for lots of them this was the first time they ever felt like they had a right to speak—and even though they might have lost this battle. . . . Well, you lose 100% of the battles you choose not to fight."

CHAPTER 15

Participatory Assessment in a Climate of Accountability

*Daniel Hickey, Michelle Honeyford,
and Jenna McWilliams*

Test-based accountability is perhaps the biggest obstacle for teachers who want to use tools like the *Teachers' Strategy Guide* (*TSG*). A decade of No Child Left Behind has driven many schools from such innovations. Instead, more students face weeks of dreary preparation for tests based on long lists of isolated concepts and basic skills, getting ready for so-called interim assessments. As argued forcefully elsewhere in this volume, basic reading and writing skills and broad-domain knowledge are crucial for success in the digital networks that are becoming central to youth's economic, social, and civic lives. Unfortunately, continuing efforts to raise achievement test scores *directly* don't foster these skills and knowledge in ways that are useful in networked contexts.

Meanwhile, policy makers and administrators insist that all educational innovations be proved to affect achievement scores in strict experimental studies. For reasons that can be surprisingly complicated, it is difficult to obtain such evidence of success for most innovations in typical schools. Participatory innovations like the *TSG* work by transforming the culture of entire classrooms, communities, and schools. While these transformations can and do leave behind broadly useful individual knowledge of academic topics, they do so somewhat indirectly—a problem for traditional models of testing and evaluation.

Fortunately, new ideas about assessment, testing, and accountability from the learning sciences and elsewhere offer new responses to these challenges. This chapter describes how we tapped some of these ideas to redesign and assess the *TSG*'s activities through a collaboration supported by the MacArthur Foundation's *21st Century Assessment Project* and encouraged by that project's leader, James Paul Gee. In the process, we developed three assessment design principles that support participatory learning:

- use contexts to give meaning to concepts and skills;
- assess reflections rather than artifacts; and
- downplay assessments and isolate tests.

This chapter describes the context of our collaboration, our research methods, and the three assessment design principles roughly in the order that they emerged.

OUR RESEARCH CONTEXT AND RESEARCH TEAM

In 2008, Daniel was invited to work with New Media Literacies (NML) to help evaluate the *TSG* curriculum. Jenna McWilliams, working at NML, oversaw the *TSG*'s development. Jenna, who had an MFA in creative writing and teaching experience in rhetoric and composition, brought a passion for social justice and equity to the project. Daniel began working with Jenna to create classroom assessments, while recruiting a local teacher, Becky Rupert, who could implement and help refine the *TSG* activities. A third participant, Michelle Honeyford, was a doctoral candidate in literacy, culture, and language education. For several years, Michelle's undergraduate English education students had been working one on one with students in Becky's writing classes. Our fourth researcher, Katie Clinton, had earned a doctorate in education and collaborated with Henry Jenkins on the 2006 NML white paper (Jenkins et al., 2009) and then the subsequent book version.

As a teacher at Aurora Alternative High School for many years, Becky was passionate about teaching students who had not thrived in mainstream public education. She had completed advanced graduate work in English literature, and was certified by the National Board for Professional Teaching Standards. She was a soft-spoken leader who had built a culture of trust with her students, many of whom had proved challenging for other teachers. But they all faced the same graduation test as the rest of the state's high school students. Becky describes her teaching goals and concerns in this book's introduction: She knew *Moby-Dick* consistently finds its way onto the list of the "most hated books," and many of her students struggled with academic reading and writing.

OUR RESEARCH DESIGN

While the development of curriculum and assessments was central to this work, neither of these products was our primary result. Because we wanted to uncover principles that would help others address the challenges surrounding participatory learning more broadly, we used a method called design-based research (DBR). DBR is not basic research that builds fundamental theories. Nor is DBR applied research testing the usefulness of fundamental theories. Rather DBR involves what are sometimes called intermediate-level theories about issues of interest in the social sciences. These principles are developed and refined in contexts similar to those where they are intended to be used and are shared with other innovators who can then further refine them. In this way, DBR focuses on useful principles and inspiring examples to help refine local theory.

Our research was particularly informed by the participatory approach to DBR described by Paul Cobb and colleagues in 2003. Consistent with their approach, our theorizing was organized around "trajectories" of shared participation. Rather than theorizing about what was happening in the minds of individual students, we focused on the collective meaning-making occurring through the interactions between Becky and her students as they were shaped by the *TSG* and other resources we were creating.

OUR INITIAL GOAL OF ASSESSING AND EVALUATING TSG

Prior research had created new kinds of formative assessments for inquiry-oriented multimedia software and educational video games (e.g., Hickey, Zuiker, Taasoobshirazi, Schafer, & Michael, 2006; Hickey, Ingram-Goble, & Jameson, 2009; Taasoobshirazi, Zuiker, Anderson, & Hickey, 2006). These assessments were different from typical formative assessments that are graded by a teacher who then provides feedback to students. Instead, students worked in small groups using detailed explanations of the reasoning behind each item to informally review their completed assessments and discuss their solutions. Generally speaking then, our initial goal was something like this:

> **Initial overall goal:** First create informal (ungraded) and formal (graded) assessments for the *TSG* activities. Then iteratively refine the informal assessments to improve performance on the formal assessments. Once students are doing well on the formal assessments, evaluate the impact of the *TSG* on external achievement tests.

These refinements were intended to eventually lead indirectly (but dramatically) to increased scores on an external achievement test that was independent of the curriculum.

Given the fact that she taught students who struggled with academic reading and writing, it was risky for Becky and the other educators who tested the *TSG* to implement a curriculum that was participatory (rather than prescriptive), focused on the social and communal (rather than the individual), and contextual and dialogic (rather than the decontextualized and didactic). By designing assessment models and examples of practice for the *TSG* that would support students' rich engagement in sophisticated literacy practices in ways that would help them succeed on state tests, we hoped to support teachers who were looking for viable ways to foster participatory learning in their classrooms. We assumed that any improvements and evidence we gathered would likely apply to most other high school English classrooms. The themes that emerged from this DBR illustrated the productive tensions that occur when fostering participatory culture within the confines of 19th-century classrooms and 20th-century tests.

WORK PHASES, EMERGENT GOALS, AND ASSESSMENT DESIGN PRINCIPLES

Our research evolved across the 3 trimesters of one school year. The 3 trimesters generally involved *implementation* (of the draft *TSG* activities and specific assessment features), *experimentation* (with different assessment design features that emerged in the first phase), and *evaluation* (of the impact of those activities on more formal assessments and test items) (Hickey et al., 2006).

These phases were aligned with Becky's development of courses for her students. In the first trimester, she offered two English classes, focusing on the first two units of the *TSG* (*Motives for Reading* and *Appropriation and Remixing*). In response to requests from those students to take another course like it in the second semester, Becky designed a new course, *Moby-Dick 2*, drawing on the fourth unit in the *TSG* (*Continuities and Silences*). She also offered *Moby-Dick* 1 again for new students who expressed interest in the course. In the third trimester, Becky offered a third course in *Moby-Dick* (drawing on the unit *Negotiating Cultural Spaces*), open to both students who had already completed 1 and 2, as well as those who had just completed the first course.

Phase 1: Fostering Engagement and Embedding Reflections

Our collaboration was initiated around the first two units in the *TSG*: *Motives for Reading* and *Appropriation and Remixing*, which formed much of the content of *Moby-Dick* 1. As described in this book's other chapters, these units assumed that reading and writing—and literacy more broadly—comprise a variety of critical and creative practices. Our approach included both "old" practices (e.g., genre study, creative and persuasive writing, literary analysis) and "new" practices (e.g., remixing, fan fiction, and blogging) as social practices that can be fostered by communal engagement mediated by new digital technologies. For example, the *Appropriation and Remixing* unit explored more traditional concepts like *audience* and *genre* and the difference between creative expression and plagiarism, but it did so in the context of new media practices like *remixing* and *transmedia navigation*. Some of the activities involved close reading of manuscript pages. Others involved the Mixed Magic Theatre's contemporary remix *Moby-Dick: Then and Now* and the music video for MC Lars's "Ahab."

Building on the prior science education work, we reviewed the *TSG* activities to identify the focal literacy practices and the more specific concepts and skills these practices called for. Then we drafted slightly more formal activities that would encourage the students and the teachers to discuss appropriate use of the underlying skills and concepts. We designed these informal assessments to prompt students and teachers to discuss (1) how traditional concepts and skills were relevant in new media contexts and (2) how the new media literacies were relevant to traditional literacy contexts.

Foster Productive Disciplinary Engagement. This first unit introduced the notions of genre and audience by showing how themes of *Moby-Dick* had been adopted across many different media genres to

appeal to very different audiences. By drawing on popular culture examples, the *TSG* aimed to help students appreciate how *Moby-Dick* helped
define the popular genre of the adventure novel and why the 19th-century
novel continues to be relevant today. But the use of MC Lars's music video
also invited students to bring in popular opinions and biases. For example,
one student insistently—and quite disruptively—slammed MC Lars in favor of nerdcore rival MC Chris. (The motivational implications of this
incident are explored in Hickey, 2011.) While some of the students appre-
ciated the activity's academic goals, many clearly viewed it as a time to express their passions about popular culture. It took several class periods to
finally get students on track by shifting the discussion to consider how an
implicit appreciation of genre was itself responsible for the rivalry between
the two musicians.

Our understanding of this event was shaped by the writings of the cognitive scientist James Greeno. As a leading proponent of "situative" theories
of knowing and learning, Greeno helped us appreciate how the *context* in
which an abstract *concept* is used (i.e., the "situation" in situative theory)
is what ultimately gives the concept meaning. Rather than being understood in the abstract, ideas like *audience* and *genre* can be thought of as
"conceptual tools" that take their meaning from the context in which they
are used (Greeno, 1998). This approach helped us appreciate that notions
like *audience* and *genre* were really abstract ideas for students, and were far
less meaningful and interesting to most of them than the features of the
popular media in which they were immersed. Before we could get students
to discuss these abstract ideas and their use in different contexts, we had
to get them to "pick up" these ideas—these "conceptual tools"—and start
using them meaningfully in the first place.

The *TSG* assumed that contemporary popular media was an ideal context for appreciating more specialized disciplinary ideas. But its use of popular culture presented a familiar dilemma: References to popular culture
encourage some students to talk about anything *but* the disciplinary ideas.
The more specific goal that began emerging at this stage was something
like this:

> **First specific goal:** Ensure that all students initially "pick up" the
> disciplinary ideas in a personally meaningful context, and then
> consider how those ideas take on different meanings in a range of
> different contexts.

Important insights for meeting this goal came from recent efforts to apply situative theories of learning to assessment (e.g., Gee, 2003a; Greeno & Gresalfi, 2008; Hickey & Anderson, 2007). The much broader view of learning in situative theories blurs the distinction between curriculum and assessment. From this perspective, *all* learning involves assessment. When students are engaging in classroom activities, they are assessing their action against *some* criteria—even if their goal is "convincing my classmates I am right" or "doing enough to get by." And even if they are learning how to get away with disrupting the class or to complete the activities without working hard, they are still learning. We needed a way to foster from the start a participatory culture where the class was assessing whether they were engaging productively with disciplinary ideas that would be meaningful in other contexts.

Embed Increasingly Formal Context x Concept Reflections. In order to foster this specific kind of disciplinary engagement, we began embedding reflection questions directly into the activities. But we structured the reflection prompts very carefully. We assumed that some of the students might not have had enough prior academic experience with the targeted concepts to give them meaning. So the initial reflections were worded to simply draw attention to the fact that the concept of genre was significant to the activity. For example, in the context of viewing the *Ahab* video, the class was asked, "Does anyone recognize any particular genre or type of narrative?"

We discouraged Becky from explaining the literary meaning of *genre* at the outset, or even engaging in extended discussion of that notion with more experienced students. Doing so could replace the goal of students' picking up and meaningfully using this conceptual tool with the goal of students' memorizing a definition of the word *genre* well enough to restate it on an assessment or recognize it on an achievement test. A more sophisticated discussion involving the whole class needed to wait until all the students had sufficient shared experience to participate in the conversation, or at least follow along meaningfully.

The initial reflections were intended to make the purpose of the activity more explicit to students, and thus the shared experience provided sufficient context for the students to meaningfully discuss how the idea of genre could take on different meanings in different contexts. Slightly more formal reflections encouraged the students to "pool" their intelligences (drawn from the activity but also from prior and related experiences) to refine their idea of genre in this context: "Can anyone see how genre is being used to appeal to particular audiences?" Although the use of informal reflection questions may sound like common classroom assessment practice, we believe we are suggesting something different. These assessment design features were not intended to assess whether each student understood the idea of genre. Rather, they were intended to foster a participatory space for productively making shared meaning of disciplinary ideas. Rather than introducing the concept of genre as an abstraction, in a historical or literary context, we used new media contexts (where we wanted our students to succeed in the future) to help students appreciate the more conventional and abstract meaning of traditional language arts concepts and skills (that our students surely encounter in subsequent high-stakes achievement tests and some future educational contexts). Over time, these insights emerged as the first principle of what we came to call *participatory assessment:*

> **First specific assessment principle: Let contexts that give meaning to concepts and skills.** This means fostering increasingly sophisticated reflections on the way that different contexts (activities, artifacts, domains, roles, etc.) reveal different meanings of valued concepts and skills. Doing so can foster a participatory culture that leaves behind individual knowledge and that will confidently transfer to other contexts (including, but not limited to, assessments and tests).

As Jenna and others were revising drafts of the various activities, Daniel and Michelle searched for opportunities to embed such prompts. We described to Becky the kinds of interactions we were hoping to foster, and then we listened and watched as she tried out the activities, first to see if the class was picking up and using the ideas, and then to see if they were using these ideas appropriately in this context. Building on the informal *discussion* of these ideas, we then aimed to foster a participatory culture around slightly more formal *writing* about these ideas in and around the artifacts that students were creating.

Phase 2: Rethinking Portfolio Assessment and Adding Artifact Reflections

Most *TSG* activities result in some sort of *artifact*—some product, created by students, that has been imbued with meaning. Many students experience many of their school assignments as meaningless exercises; they just go through the motions, especially in domains like mathematics that can easily be reduced to memorized procedures. In this context, Katie Clinton helped us appreciate Deborah Brandt's (2009) argument that the explosion of digital networks has made writing central to 21st-century mass literacy in the same way that the explosion of print made reading central to 20th-century mass literacy. This reality and the multimodal writing in the various *TSG* activities reveal the absurdity of the 21st-century skills movement. The widespread efforts to standardize, teach, and test new skills ultimately involve very little authentic writing. It can be expensive and time-consuming to assess writing—particularly when that writing is meaningful and multi-modal (Hickey, Honeyford, Clinton, & McWilliams, 2010). The problems of assessing and testing writing present perhaps the largest challenge for expanding opportunities for participatory learning within public education. The highly structured writing tasks on standardized tests have pushed much secondary writing instruction to focus on standardized forms, such as the five-paragraph essay. Such structured "knowledge telling" has very little to do with the "knowledge construction" that is central to the work of experienced writers. Another incident in Becky's class helped catalyze our thinking about possible solutions to this problem.

Use Participatory Culture to Rethink Portfolio Assessment. One activity in the *TSG*'s first unit focuses on annotating (adding references and extending) and ornamenting (adding embellishments and flourishes) as participatory social practices that help readers understand and connect with texts. Our early work in designing initial reflections for this activity had prompted a productive initial discussion among Becky's students. Annotating and ornamenting *Moby-Dick*'s first chapter helped students uncover interesting and amusing nuances, such as the reference in Chapter 1 of the book to flatulence and the "Pythagorean maxim" (which tells us to "avoid beans"):

> For as in this world, head winds are far more prevalent than winds from astern (that is, if you never violate the Pythagorean maxim), so for the most part the Commodore on the quarter-deck gets his atmosphere at second hand from the sailors on the forecastle.

This activity also provided a meaningful context for viewing online videos in which Melville scholar Wyn Kelley and others describe their own annotation and ornamentation practices. More formal reflections in the activity prompted students to consider the nuanced differences between the two practices.

The emerging participatory feel of this activity began to fade, however, when the students were asked to reproduce their annotations and ornamentations on transparencies and present them to the class. Students began asking for very specific examples of "good" annotations and ornamentation, seeking very specific feedback ("Is *this* what you want???"). By the day that students presented their artifacts, the participatory and formative intent of the activity had shifted to a much more individual and summative one. The results were really *boring*! Students walked through their annotations; some seemed embarrassed by the same ornamentations that they had been showing off to their group just a few days before. The second remarkable thing was how *disruptive* students became as group after group went to the front of the room to read their texts. Becky ended up referring more students to the principal's office that day than she typically did in an entire school year.

Our interpretation of this event was shaped by the characterization of participatory culture presented in NML's white paper on media education in the 21st century (Jenkins et al., 2009). For NML, a participatory culture is one where "not every member must contribute, but all must believe they are free to contribute when ready and that what they contribute will be appropriately valued" (p. 7). Arguably, at least some aspects of this culture were in place during the annotation and ornamentation activities. Given a very open-ended assignment, students seemed to naturally ask each other for help. Most important, students were relatively free to engage with their classmates in whatever manner suited them for the purpose of the activity. This was certainly *not* the case with the presentation or with most other classroom assessments. The very premise of formal classroom assessments is that students *must* contribute to them in a very structured way and at a set time.

The students' worries about being evaluated helped us realize that directly assessing the artifacts they created was undermining our efforts to foster participatory learning. But in most formal school contexts, most teachers would insist on and most students would need some sort of accountability associated with the artifacts that they produced. The specific goal that emerged here was something like this:

> **Second specific goal:** Find strategies for assessing student artifacts and portfolios that foster rather than undermine participatory culture.

Our efforts to meet this goal were helped by prior research on portfolio assessment. For example, in 1997, James Popham had cautioned against "dysfunctionally detailed" (p. 98) rubrics. This helped us appreciate that assessing students' artifacts naturally leads students to expect—and teachers to provide—specific examples and overly detailed rubrics of what "teachers want." Indeed the prospect of formally presenting their annotations and ornamentations to the class and visitors led students to worry more about how their artifacts looked and less about how the strategies had helped them comprehend the text, or consider, for example, the contexts in which annotation might be more appropriate than ornamentation, and vice versa.

Additional insights came from a 2007 paper by Lawrence Habib and Line Wittek called The Portfolio as Artifact and Actor. It applied situative theories of learning to portfolio assessment and helped us theorize the participatory potential of portfolios. The title refers to the way portfolios and other artifacts of learning "act" to take on meaning. Artifacts should take on a role that reflects their social and technological context; they may take on a life of their own, be used in ways they were not intended, and shape the actions of other learners or the artifacts they produce. This, in turn, helped us appreciate the distinction that Dysthe, Engelsen, and Lima (2007) made between *working portfolios* and *presentation portfolios*. Working portfolios act out a more formative role, trying out different ways of representing knowledge and learning, somewhat akin to acting classes. Presentation portfolios act out a more finished role, akin to a signature performance. While the activities in the *TSG* envisioned more of the former, even informal assessments of the artifacts by the teacher made it more of the latter. We gradually came to realize that the reflections that we had been embedding in the activities pointed to a strategy for meeting this goal.

Adding Artifact Reflections. The strategy for balancing assessment needs around student artifacts had students write a reflection about how their artifact showed that they had engaged with the relevant disciplinary ideas—and had the teacher grade those reflections instead of the artifacts themselves. While reflections are well established in the portfolio assessment literature, we were thinking about them differently. What we came to call "artifact reflections" were more formal versions of the "activity reflections" that we had been embedding into the *TSG*. Rather than grading the annotations and ornamentations that students were creating directly, we asked them to include reflections that explained how their artifacts illustrated the "big ideas" of the activity. For example, we asked students, "How do your creations show why you would annotate instead of ornament?"

These reflections were "semiformal" in that they were written and formally evaluated. But they (a) were similar to the informal reflections they encountered previously; (b) were completed alongside the creation of the artifact; and (c) were generously evaluated, with full points given for any coherent response.

As we tried out different artifact reflections, we began to realize that aligning the informal activity reflections and the semiformal artifact reflections let us refine and raise our expectations for student artifacts. For example, it is quite a challenge for students to annotate and ornament a manuscript page in a way that directly demonstrates they understand the differences between the two practices and when one would be more appropriate than the other. It would also be quite difficult for a teacher to reliably assess an artifact on those terms. By off-loading most of the summative assessment functions from the artifacts, the reflections allowed the artifacts to take on a range of more authentic roles. These insights became the second principle of participatory assessment:

> **Second specific assessment principle: Assess reflections rather than artifacts.** Artifacts students create in classrooms should not be directly evaluated by teachers or peers. Doing so undermines participation and agency. Rather, have students reflect on their process, building on informal reflections that were embedded in the activity.

As we experimented with the principle, we learned that carefully worded reflection prompts invite individuals to reveal their understanding of valued concepts and skills without turning exciting activities into humdrum assignments. We saw students start writing their reflections, then go back and revise their artifacts, and then revise their reflections again. We learned that it was relatively easy for teachers to assess each student's "understanding" of the disciplinary ideas, because it was impossible for individuals to reflect on those ideas meaningfully if they had not already been engaging with them meaningfully (Hickey, McWilliams, & Honeyford, 2011).

Artifact reflections can serve as the primary and even solitary evidence for many classroom accountability functions, *as long as they are used in a participatory context.* If they are simply tacked on to a traditional writing assignment, they just turn into another exam item, and encourage students to provide abstract definitions. In this case, students' written responses to the reflection certainly provided some useful evidence for Becky and for us. But the formative value of the reflections (for improving writing) and summative value (for assessing writing proficiency) were enhanced when they were embedded in the participatory fabric of the activity. Rather than serving as yet another quiz item, they need to be presented *and taken up* as tools that help everyone participate in the knowledge practices of the activity. This is easiest when the reflections are drafted, discussed, and assessed as slightly more formal versions of the reflective discourse prompted by the informal reflections during the activity.

Phase 3: Protecting Participation and Evaluating at a Distance

Obviously, accomplishing our goal of indirectly affecting external achievement while fostering a participatory culture would ultimately require *evidence* of achievement. The prior science education research that informed this work had obtained statistically meaningful gains on "standards-oriented" (i.e., "external") achievement tests only after obtaining substantial gains on formal "curriculum-oriented" classroom assessments. In our usage, formal classroom assessments need to have sufficient structure that they

1. can be completed before and after instruction;
2. are independent of student-produced artifacts; and
3. can be scored reliably.

In measurement terms, the prior studies had shown that average scores on formal classroom assessments needed to increase at least one standard deviation before that learning was "echoed" in statistically significant gains on external achievement test items that were aligned to external standards but unrelated to the curriculum. Thus, the specific assessment and testing goal that we brought into the project went something like this:

Third specific goal: Obtain substantial gains (at least one standard deviation) on formal classroom assessments, then evaluate the overall impact of the entire curriculum on external achievement test items aligned with relevant educational standards but independent of the particular curriculum.

However, the prior studies had shown that informal and semiformal assessments (like our activity and artifact reflections) needed to be working well before we could expect substantial gains on the formal classroom assessment. In those studies it had also taken 2 years to obtain those gains.

As Jenna McWilliams describes earlier in this book, Becky's school, and thus our collaboration, were upended by the funding cuts of 2009. Just as we began expanding our collaboration to include other teachers at Aurora, the district announced that the school would be closed. While we had made a lot of progress, we were still figuring out the artifact reflections and had just begun thinking about formal classroom assessments.

Not knowing what the future held, we elected to accelerate our plans and add formal assessment and test items at the end of the activities and modules. For example, we added a formal essay item to the annotation and ornamentation activity that asked students to "describe a situation where annotation would be more appropriate than ornamentation." We also added in some released free response writing items from the College Board's Advanced Placement test in English literature that were aligned to the most relevant state English language arts standards.

Even though we warned Becky that these items would be very hard for her students, she was *very* disappointed in their performance. And many of her students were also disappointed. They took it quite personally. Their disappointment was particularly salient to us in light of how successful the *TSG* had been in fostering a participatory culture in that same classroom. But we also knew that few innovators would be blessed with the multiyear opportunity that the MacArthur Foundation had so generously provided us. We concluded that a lot remains to be learned in this regard.

We took away several lessons from this experience. Some of these lessons concerned formal classroom assessments. We remained confident that carefully aligned activity and event reflections would allow for very high expectations on formal classroom assessments. And we also remained confident that challenging formal assessments were essential to continued refinement of the activities and semiformal assessments. But we also knew that students and teachers expect that most students who have engaged meaningfully in classroom activities will get near the highest score possible on classroom assessments. If we had elected to have students complete some of the formal assessment items as a pretest *before* the unit, the class would have naturally focused more on how far they had come. As long as the teacher did not explain the complete answers to the curriculum's big questions at that time, the class could refer back to their initial uncertainty to appreciate their progress. We were able to implement this strategy in the third course and it seemed a promising solution.

Like many teachers, Becky wanted to review students' completed formal writing assessments with her students in order to clarify and provide feedback. While we did not discourage her, we suspected that doing so would not be particularly useful considering that we had focused more on reading rather than the ideas and practices of analytical writing. Discussing those ideas and practices in the abstract context of the assessment also is likely to encourage students who were struggling to simply memorize the abstract definition. The lesson here is that formal assessments need to be treated more as an evaluation of the curriculum than an evaluation of the students. Although we found little compelling evidence that writing had improved, performance on the open-ended items showed evidence of improved reading comprehension and understanding of analysis. This suggested that these activities *were* promising and that Becky and her class *had* done a good job enacting them.

This incident also taught us some lessons about external achievement testing. For reasons beyond the scope of this chapter, it is remarkably difficult to measure the achievement impact of modules or even entire curricula. But as researchers, we need to do so. Any achievement testing needs to be entirely isolated from the process of designing and enacting the curriculum. Our concerns about classroom assessments and external tests came together in our third principle:

> *Third specific assessment principle: Downplay assessments and isolate tests*. Participatory classroom culture should be protected from the abstract and individual representations of knowledge on formal classroom assessments. Such assessments should be used more for evaluating and refining curriculum than for comparing individual learning and providing individual feedback. Teaching, curriculum, and classroom assessments should be isolated from external achievement tests and their narrow caricatures of knowledge; such tests should be used only by researchers at a distance to gather comparison data, predict impact, and measure improvement over time.

We are particularly excited about the ways that newly available technology can help accomplish this goal. For example, we are now using Google Forms to make simple web-based testlets with released multiple-choice test items that let us easily estimate the impact of a module on student achievement. This offers a simple way to gather this information while keeping teachers from inadvertently teaching to the test items (which renders them meaningless).

SUBSEQUENT EFFORTS AND NEXT STEPS

While the abrupt closure of Aurora Alternative High School certainly disrupted our efforts, we made substantial progress toward addressing the assessment and testing challenges described in the introduction. Becky was reassigned to a high school that was part of the New Tech network of project-based learning (PBL) schools. While the *TSG* was not sufficiently aligned with the New Tech model to use in that school, Daniel and Jenna continued working with Becky to create new PBL modules. They found that the insights about participatory learning and assessment that came from this project were helpful for thinking about designing "participatory PBL."

Since this project there has been continued effort to establish a modest self-sustaining professional development network that includes Becky and a handful of other local English teachers. The network has resulted in a number of new curricular modules that incorporate NML's ideas about participatory learning and our ideas about participatory assessment. With the help of a new doctoral students, Rebecca Itow, some of this work is taking place within the Digital Is network sponsored by the National Writing Project (NWP) and we are hoping to expand our network to other NWP teachers.

Our modest success seems promising in light of the disappointment many of us feel about the handful of programs that have been proven to affect external achievement in randomized studies, according to the U.S. Department of Education's What Works Clearinghouse. Fortunately, this "gold standard" for "evidence-based curriculum" may lose its relevance within major assessment reforms now under way in the United States. But it does seem to us that some evidence on externally developed tests will always be demanded for most educational innovations. We hope that this chapter will help other developers and innovators obtain such evidence in ways that ultimately enhance participatory culture in schools, homes, informal learning networks, or wherever learning occurs in the future.

Conclusion

Reimagining and Reinventing the English Classroom for the Digital Age

Jenna McWilliams and Katie Clinton

The driving purpose of the *Teachers' Strategy Guide* (*TSG*), and by extension this book, was to consider strategies for transforming the domain of English education to support learners' engagement with an increasingly participatory culture. In a truly participatory culture, we all get to decide what matters—not just corporations, not just school boards, not just elites—everybody. But that means we need to equip everybody with the tools, sensibilities, and proficiencies to participate. It's necessary but no longer sufficient to train learners to think like fledgling literary scholars; we must also prepare them to engage more broadly in conversations about transforming their lives and, in the process, the role of reading and writing in their communities and cultures.

In creating the *TSG*, the New Media Literacies (NML) team, collectively, spent hundreds—perhaps even thousands—of hours developing, critiquing, and refining content. The researchers thought hard about the kind of classroom they hoped to see and the kind of learners that they hoped would emerge. *TSG* activities emphasized what NML believes is best about print-based and new media literacies.

BRINGING THE TSG TO SCHOOL

Well. What is it that they say about the best-laid plans of mice and media scholars?

As any experienced teacher can attest, there exists a gap—sometimes narrow, sometimes too wide to see across—between what we plan for any given class and what ultimately happens. The principles listed below emerged out of moments of surprise, confusion, and unexpected success.

Frederick Erickson (1984) once noted that the organization for learning is *part* of the content learned. Seeking to reconfigure the organization for learning in the English classroom, NML created a design experiment using Pierre Lévy's (1997) concept of collective intelligence—the ability to pool knowledge and compare notes with others toward a common goal. By applying the concept of collective intelligence to the English classroom NML created a problem space for exploring what learning in the classroom could look like if organized by new forms of collective information-processing and knowledge-building. By using collective intelligence as a mechanism (occurring on many levels) for fostering a participatory dynamic in the English classroom, NML hoped to interrupt the "social gravity" (Gee, 1998) of traditionally defined norms, roles, and organizational structures.

In designing the guide, the team began by asking, "What is reading in a participatory culture?" The *TSG* became a first attempt at answering this question. Then, when NML entered classrooms to observe the guide in use, the researchers quickly saw that participatory ideals must be accompanied by a participatory *approach* to teaching and learning. NML's fieldwork demonstrated that collective intelligence was largely missing from American educational practice; it was far more common to hear an exhortation to "keep your eyes on your own paper" than to "pool your background knowledge to figure out what this sentence means"; far more likely to hear a teacher warn students away from Wikipedia than to help students correct the inaccuracies contained on a Wikipedia page.

RECONSIDERING CORE DESIGN QUESTIONS

The design questions below—call them provocations for participatory practices—mark trouble spots: issues and moments that had NML struggling to see the working whole of the classroom, and the role of the *TSG* curriculum as one part of that larger system. As such, they signify some of the simultaneous changes to the system NML is advocating. This discussion of these design themes is anchored in stories from the field. These research moments are chosen to help us think about how a collective intelligence model can provide a beginning place for figuring out the new sorts of logics, rule sets, skills sets, and values that can make the English classroom a new kind of knowledge community.

1. How Do We Create a Community of Readers in the English Classroom?

For teachers who want to build a collaborative, participatory community of readers, the challenges are legion. Schools are bound by the often conflicting demands of preparing learners for success in the 21st century while simultaneously preparing them for success in the standardized testing system that dominates our No Child Left Behind–era schooling structure. This structure is built on what Paulo Freire (1970/2009) has called a "banking" approach to education: We fill kids up with facts and pieces of knowledge that we hope they can then retrieve during high-stakes assessment moments. We want them to be able to find Iraq on a map, just in case they find themselves in a situation that requires it. And when they are unable to complete this task on demand, we label young people as members of "the dumbest generation" (Bauerlein, 2008; Tapscott, 2009). Never mind that if you sit most young people down in front of a networked computer and ask them to find Iraq on a map, they'll quickly retrieve a host of options. Do you want a satellite picture? A weather map? A street map? Perhaps a map indicating areas of most intense fighting?

By the time kids get to high school, they've been well versed in the penalties for collaboration; pooling resources with classmates, no matter how productive, is often referred to as "cheating." Students are also often confused: They know for sure that plagiarism is grounds for punishment, yet their online communities are filled with examples of people repurposing and remixing the work of others. Instead of learning how to creatively and ethically appropriate media content, they learn never to use the copy-and-paste functions on their computers. It's no wonder that so many teachers report confronting a student over plagiarism concerns and being met with blank stares.

NML's goal, then, was to create a "community of learners" (Brown, 1992) governed and motivated by an ethos that is distinctly different from the spirit that characterizes traditional classroom structures. As conceptual touchstones for creating a new kind of knowledge culture in the classroom, the project used Pierre Lévy's related concepts of collective intelligence and of knowledge communities. Within a knowledge community, "no one knows everything, everyone knows something, all knowledge resides in humanity" (Lévy, 1997, pp. 13–14). Lévy believes that it is through small, local experiments that we will learn to live within knowledge communities. We need to prepare learners to recognize, retrieve, contribute to, and take ownership of the knowledge that circulates within distributed networks.

Offering a compelling example of a new mindset for guiding reading, Jenkins suggests that reading can be like a field trip to the zoo. At the zoo everyone notices different things. And upon returning everyone talks about what he or she saw. Instead of the school mindset where knowing what happened at the zoo is a matter of guessing the teacher's interpretations of the class's zoo trip, a collective intelligence mindset creates understanding of what happened at the zoo through information exchange, as students share their personal experiences, and, perhaps, too, through deliberation or debate, as people offer potentially contradictory information ("There were two giraffes." "No, three!").

What would it mean to read a book like *Moby-Dick* in this way? Instead of seeking to converge with a canonical interpretation—a situation where, in theory, everyone is trying to participate in the same way, with the same information—the idea would be that readers would experience the book in a way that matches their passions and interests, and thus everyone would take a unique trajectory through the book and everyone would have unique observations to share.

2. How Do We Break Down the Expert Paradigm?

The institution of schooling was designed around the premise that knowledge was a scarce commodity: In order for cultural information and literacies to pass through the generations, we needed a system whereby teachers, who possess the key information, can hand it down to students. Assessment practices—including testing and grading—have developed to support this model. The students who best retain and reproduce key information (dates, math formulas, and the like) earn the highest test scores.

This scarcity model is collapsing beneath the weight of information abundance. Increasingly, information and expertise are spread across a broad network of people and tools, and increasingly widespread access to networked technologies means that, in theory at least, the same information is available to everybody. In such a world, knowing how to find, process, and exchange already known knowledge (knowledge that is the product of the expert paradigm) is as important as knowing how to work together, deliberate, debate, argue, and create knowledge (knowledge that is a product of the collective intelligence paradigm).

NML uses the notion of *distributed expertise* as a contrast with the more traditional expert paradigm. The expert paradigm assumes a static, bounded body of knowledge; in this model, expertise is hierarchical and generally brokered by credentialed authorities (Jenkins, 2006a). When the expert paradigm was an accurate way of thinking about how knowledge is built and passed on, the process of pouring information into the brains of students made more sense: Since most of the world's cumulative knowledge could not be readily or easily obtained on short notice, information needed to be stored in the heads of individuals.

In contrast, the notion of distributed expertise assumes that knowledge is spread across a diffuse network of people and tools. Operating within this model involves developing a capacity for obtaining and meaningfully acting on different kinds of expertise. Working against the grain of the traditional conception of the teacher-students relationship, the banking approach in which students are the passive recipients of the teacher's knowledge, NML shares Pavlo Freire's conclusion that ideally "the teacher is no longer merely the-one-who-teaches, but one who is [him- or herself] taught in dialogue with the students, who in turn while being taught also teach" (Freire, 1970/2009, p. 80). From this view, the classroom is envisioned as a site where new knowledge, grounded in the experiences of students and teachers alike, is produced through meaningful dialogue (Freire's dialogical method), and different types of knowledge are valued at different times.

This protean view of expertise rejects the traditionally defined hierarchical relationships between the teacher and students. Instead, "teacher and learner roles are not fixed positions but change continuously" (Lund & Rasmussen, 2010, p. 4065). Introducing an epistemological pluralism into the English language arts classroom requires students and teachers alike to learn to "collaborate by difference" (Davidson, 2008), a form of co-participation that calls for very different skills from those developed by learning organized by a paradigm of converging-on-the-already-known.

In future iterations of this study, this design principle might push researchers to further consider the notion of collective intelligence as it plays out on the individual level. What are the skills related to information processing and knowledge building necessary for thriving in a collective intelligence system? Eventually, it might be fruitful to think about the ELA classroom as a place where the "content" to be learned is vitally connected to learning to think, act, react, debate, deliberate, problem solve, innovate, and collaborate in a networked world.

Many of the teachers, seeking to create a more open environment that respected multiple forms of expertise and different motives for reading, encounter what researcher Daniel T. Hickey labeled the "Is this what you want?" phenomenon (Hickey et al., 2011, p. 257). For many students, school experiences have led to a passive approach to learning—a form of "learned helplessness" (Maier & Seligman, 1976). This is not laziness; today's students are as willing to work hard as were any of their predecessors. But the same school systems that position students as receptacles for the teacher's knowledge also position teachers as the arbiters of what counts as achievement. The requirements for success feel mysterious to many students, perhaps especially for those students who have had experiences in participatory cultures outside school.

3. How Do We Support a Culture of Increased Generativity?

Traditionally, reading and writing have been treated as separate practices, requiring different skill sets and proficiencies. Digital technologies support a new relationship between these practices. Addressing this new relationship between reading and writing, literary scholar Deborah Brandt (2009) notes that we are entering a second stage of mass literacy. In the first stage, reading was key and identified as a universal right. In this second stage, writing has become increasingly dominant and valuable, and she notes that our institutions are not equipped to handle this shift. Offering a complementary vision of reading in a new media age, in a report from the National Council of Teachers of English, Kathleen Yancey notes, "Society has focused on children as readers because, historically, it has been much more interested in children as receptors than as producers of the written word" (2009, p. 2). What happens when both reading and writing become the grounds for the literary mind?

While piloting the *TSG* in her classroom at Aurora High School in Indiana, and hoping to take advantage of the new possibilities for interaction and expression afforded by social networking tools, Becky Rupert created a social networking site for her students. Use of the site, as Becky explained, had such a transformative effect on her classroom that we decided to invite students from one of our other research sites to join their conversation.

As described in Chapter 2, when the new group of students logged into Becky's class's site they were told to read through the site and the profiles of the Indiana students, an that in the next classroom session they would have the opportunity to create their own profiles. But, instead of just reading through the material on the site, many of the students "jumped in" and posted sexually explicit comments to the Indiana students' profiles. Due to a technical difficulty, the students had been admitted to Becky's site using an administrator's account, so the comments to Indiana students' profiles looked like they had been made by one of the NML researchers.

This incident led to an important insight about student dispositions toward engagement with social media. The researchers had assumed that students instructed to "read through the site" would do just (and only) that—read through the site. But for the students, the act of reading the site was automatically connected with their impulse to respond to the site. (For more on this, see Barab, MaKinster, Moore, & Cunningham, 2001; Moore & Barab, 2002.)

A way to talk about the relationship between reading and writing evinced by the students is expressed by technology and social media guru Clay Shirky, who describes "what even very young children know about technology":

> I was having dinner with a group of friends, talking about our kids, and one of them told a story about watching a DVD with his four-year-old daughter. In the middle of the movie, apropos of nothing, she jumped up off the couch and ran around behind the screen. My friend thought she wanted to see if the people in the movie were really back there. But that wasn't what she was up to. She started rooting around in the cables behind the screen. Her dad asked, "What you doing?" And she stuck her head out from behind the screen and said, "Looking for the mouse." Here's what 4-year-olds know: A screen that ships without a mouse ships broken. Media that's targeted at you but doesn't include you may not be worth sitting for. (2008a)

This story suggests a way of interpreting what happened in the classroom. When we read online, we are poised to engage creatively with what we're reading in a vast variety of ways. We might engage by writing—by drafting a blogpost or a piece of creative fan fiction. But we might also engage with images, numbers, audio, or video; by working with the text's source code; by remixing; or by circulating the text to members of our social circle who we think might find it interesting. To make visible this new close relationship between reading and writing online—and the concomitant need to develop new skills and dispositions for managing the links between consuming (reading), producing (writing), and sharing—Katie Clinton and Jenna McWilliams coined the term "reading with mouse in hand."

Teachers often encourage students to read with a pencil in their hands—not simply letting the words pass over their eyeballs but critically engaging with them, taking notes, asking questions, critiquing as they go. When students read with a mouse in their hands, they take this idea one step further: They assume that they must actively respond to what's been put in front of them; they are poised to participate; they (need to) take responsibility over the quality of information and correct it publicly if it is wrong.

Reading with mouse in hand is a qualitatively different act from reading with pencil in hand, a common practice among professional writers and voracious readers. The difference is in what happens to the generative activity linked to one's reading. When you are reading with mouse in hand, your writing is going public instantly in a way that marginalia never could. Reading with mouse in hand, therefore, is a practice that requires a deep sense of an intended public, which is much broader than the public generally identified by the school context.

Contributing to participatory culture is now only a mouse click away. Bridging the participation gap requires teaching mindsets, skill sets, and ethical sets that address the ways that writing in the classroom can now become an ever more public activity. Reading with a mouse in hand involves fostering new dispositions that link consuming (reading), producing (writing), and sharing (circulation). One dimension of this new disposition is explained by Shirky's (2008b) identification of a "publish, then filter" approach, where everything goes live, most of it open for public consumption and appraisal, and the burden of filtering and making sense of all that generative work has been shifted away from the writer and toward the readers.

NML's fieldwork has demonstrated that working within increasingly public social spaces (such as the private network on Ning or collaborative sites like Wikipedia) has the potential to support authentic and productive participation in new media literacy practices. The challenge becomes identifying strategies for scaffolding learners as they move into these public spaces where content is less controlled and norms are less explicit.

4. How Do We Develop Participatory Assessment Structures?

Both colloquially and professionally, many stakeholders consider assessment to be any formal measure of achievement, primarily in the form of tests or essays (Delandshere, 2001). In fact, however, assessment is much more pervasive: It is a natural component of all activity systems and, as Gee (2009) points out, has its *natural home* in human action. Assessment structures, when they serve the purpose of a community, enable community members to participate in community activities in socially meaningful and personally powerful ways. Jenkins et al. describe a 17-year-old girl who taught herself to sew in order to more fully participate in fan-related cosplay (or costume play). She explains:

> The biggest payoff of cosplay is to go to the conventions where there are other people who know who you are dressed as and can appreciate your effort. At the first convention I ever went to, I must have had fifty people take my picture and at least ten of them came up and hugged me. . . . People put the pictures up on their websites after the con. So after a con, you can search for pictures of yourself and if you are lucky, you will find five or ten. (2009, pp. 29–30)

This comment captures the spirit of assessment as embedded in human activity and as supporting growth and identity-building within communities of practice. The standards that matter to her are those developed within and applied by the fan community itself. These assessment criteria are internalized through a process of experimentation and reflection; they become part of how she sees herself and her place in her community.

An important feature of many participatory cultures is that the norms and value systems of these groups are shaped by their members. As Gee (2003b) points out, many video games are especially effective not only in recruiting players into an already existing way of thinking, valuing, and behaving, but also in allowing and even encouraging players to help shape and shift those cultural norms. How strange it must be, then, for learners to find themselves in a school system in which the norms

1. were created long before they first entered the community;
2. exist, for the most part, without a clear rationale; and
3. are not open to criticism or change.

Too frequently, educational assessments are used to track and sort students instead of supporting their development and learning. Even the effort to introduce a formative assessment model has been co-opted by the demand for achievement on high-stakes tests, and has often been used as what Shepard (2007) calls "early-warning summative assessments."

For teachers who want to integrate new media technologies and accompanying new media literacies practices into their classrooms, a reconsideration of the role of assessment becomes uniquely salient: Embracing the spirit of these new practices means also embracing what Knobel and Lankshear call the new "ethos stuff"—literacy practices that are "more 'participatory,' 'collaborative,' and 'distributed' in nature than conventional literacies" (2007, p. 7). There remains an enormous tension between these practices and literacy practices as traditionally taught. Many are calling for new approaches to assessment that can bridge the gap between communally meaningful action and individual accountability (Herrington, Hodgson, & Moran, 2009, p. 200).

It's no wonder, then, that educators struggle to support student engagement in collective meaning-making sites whose structures seem so at odds with the highly individualistic attitude contemporary schooling has inherited. The rhetoric of the "dumbest generation," proposed by Mark Bauerlein (2008) and others, judges current students lacking in terms of their performance on standardized achievement measures as compared with the performances of previous generations of learners. In many cases, current assessments test for an antiquated set of proficiencies that no longer align with the emerging valued practices of an increasingly participatory culture.

Additionally, while the "ethos stuff" of online communities may *appear* incommensurate with school-based learning spaces, they are in fact potentially complementary: Informal participatory learning spaces often offer more opportunities for learning than opportunities for learners to reflect upon what they've learned; schools offer a unique site for reflection about how knowledge is produced and the value of cultural practices. Insofar as our assessment mechanisms reflect and promote the kinds of knowledge we value, we need new tools that place a premium on collaboration and participation, on knowledge sharing and information exchange, on creative repurposing, and on the capacity to innovate in response to changes in our environment. Most of our current tests measure the exact opposite criteria.

FINAL THOUGHTS

Despite its democratic and inclusive leanings, participatory culture is not immune to the hegemonic impulses of dominant cultural groups that seek to regulate who can participate and determine what kinds of contributions are valued. Any effort to introduce participatory cultures into the formal classroom simultaneously heightens the risk of containment, even as the process of spreading participatory skills helps to challenge historic efforts to constrain grassroots engagement. In part, the push toward control is a feature of an institution whose continued existence depends on a three-part response to anything that threatens its equilibrium: condemnation, co-opting, and marginalization (Collins & Halverson, 2009). The democratic rhetoric, which promises "science for all," as C. Barton (1998) and others (e.g., Giroux, 1991; Kozol, 1991) have pointed out, obscures the great extent to which schooling, in practice, supports only a "science for some" approach, maintaining the status quo even at the expense of stifling a range of other voices within the community.

New media practices can as easily be co-opted for dominant interests as they can be used to broaden the expressive space of the English classroom and offer multiple points of entry into studying literature. Writing in 1994, in the giddy early days of the digital revolution, cultural theorist John Fiske argued that "the multiplication of communication and information technologies extends the terrains of struggle, modifies the forms struggle may take, and makes it even more imperative that people grasp the opportunities for struggle that the multiplying of technologies offers" (p. 240). For Fiske, access to new media platforms and practices does not guarantee any specific outcome; it only creates new contexts within which we may battle over resources and over the infrastructure and policies shaping our participation. New media have democratic potentials, but to achieve these potentials, we need to work together to achieve the kinds of cultural diversity and democratized participation we desire.

The classroom represents a central site where this battle may be won or lost. Our hope, as it has been for so many others in the past, is that education may be the great equalizer, ensuring widespread access to the skills and tools needed for democratic citizenship. Yet there is a danger that education, working as a wing of the state, may devalue these emerging forms of participation, dismissing activities that are meaningful to students outside school, convincing them that they have little of significance to contribute to these larger conversations. There is no assurance that our culture will stay as open as it is today to diverse participants, that we will have the same level of free and easy access to channels of communication, that we will continue to expand who can create and share media.

In order to transform learning environments there is a need to suspend powerful and very much entrenched preconceptions about education. Educators need to question often taken-for-granted ways of thinking about the goals and processes of schooling: especially those premised on hierarchy, disciplines, canons, grades, standards, credentialed expertise, and control. This is not to say that traditional education is all wrong, or that it doesn't have valuable things to offer. But as educators, we need to ask anew which practices are serving the needs of our students, which students are being served, and what forms of learning are being facilitated. We all need to ask these questions about the values of traditional print literacy and we need to ask these questions about the new practices from participatory culture we might bring into our schools.

This chapter has sought to outline some of the challenges we will need to confront as we engage in the process of reimagining and reinventing schooling and especially as we all think more deeply about how to integrate the values of a more participatory culture into our educational practices. What logics, ideas, and mechanisms are sheltered under this umbrella term *participatory*? What is a participatory curriculum? What are its weaknesses and strengths? What is to be gained by creating new sorts of knowledge communities in schools? How can the traditional and the new work together? What roles can new media, teachers, students, and the public play in this reconfiguring process? We are all stakeholders in the educational system. Efforts to address these and similar questions will help usher in the next phase of research into participatory culture, digital media, and learning.

References

Since *Moby-Dick* is commonly available in many editions, we have used chapter titles and numbers throughout instead of page numbers for our references. But it is important to know that the book appeared in two different first editions (the British and the American) and that many editions collate the two without comment. The one edition that makes the differences visible is the Longman Critical Edition, edited by John Bryant and Haskell Springer, listed in the References below.

Bacon-Smith, C. (1992). *Enterprising women: Television fandom and the creation of popular myth.* Philadelphia: University of Pennsylvania Press.

Bakhtin, M. (1981). *The dialogic imagination: Four essays.* (Michael Holquist, Ed.; Caryl Emerson and Michael Holquist, Trans.). Austin: University of Texas Press.

Barab, S. A., MaKinster, J. G., Moore, J. A., & Cunningham, D. J. (2001). Designing and building an on-line community: The struggle to support sociability in the inquiry learning forum. *Educational Technology Research and Development, 49*(4), 71–96.

Bauerlein, M. (2008). *The dumbest generation: How the digital age stupefies young Americans and jeopardizes our future (or, don't trust anyone under 30).* New York: Tarcher.

Beale, T. (1839). *The natural history of the sperm whale.* London, UK: John Van Voorst.

Bender, H. (1999). *The Sandman companion.* New York: Vertigo-DC Comics.

Benkler, Y. (2007). *The wealth of networks: How social production transforms markets and freedom.* New Haven: Yale University Press.

Black, R. (2008). *Adolescents and online fan fiction.* New York: Peter Lang.

Bleich, D. (1986). Gender interests in reading and language. In E. A. Flynn & P. P. Schweickart's (Eds.), *Gender and reading: Essays on readers, texts, and contexts* (pp. 234–266). Baltimore, MD: Johns Hopkins University Press.

Bolter, J. D. (1991). *Writing space: The computer, hypertext, and the history of writing.* Hillsdale, NJ: Lawrence Erlbaum Associates.

boyd, d. (2009, February 26). Social media is here to stay . . . now what? Microsoft Research Tech Fest, Redmond, WA. Retrieved from http://www.danah.org/papers/talks/MSRTechFest2009.html

Brandt, D. (2009). *Literacy and learning: Reflections on writing, reading, and society.* San Francisco: Jossey-Bass.

Brown, A. L. (1992). Design experiments: Theoretical and methodological challenges in creating complex interventions in classroom settings. *The Journal of Learning Sciences, 2*(2), 141–178.

Brown, J. S., & Adler, R. P. (2008). Minds on fire: Open education, the long tail, and learning 2.0. *Educause Review, 43*(1), 16–32.

Brown, M. (2007). Undisciplined reading. *Common-Place, 8*(1). Retrieved from http://www.common-place.org/vol-08/no-01/reading/

Busse, K., & Hellekson, K. (2006). Work in progress. In K. Busse & K. Hellekson (Eds.), *Fan fiction and fan communities in the age of the Internet* (pp. 5–32). Jefferson, NC: McFarland.

Calabrese Barton, A. (1998). Teaching science with homeless children: Pedagogy, representation, and identity. *Journal of Research in Science Teaching, 35*(4), 379–394.

Carr, N. (2010). *The shallows: What the Internet is doing to our minds.* New York: W. W. Norton.

Center for Media Literacy. (n.d.). Five key questions form foundation for media literacy. Retrieved from http://www.medialit.org/reading_room/article677.html

Chabon, M. (2008). Fan fictions: On Sherlock Holmes. In *Maps and legends: Reading and writing along the borderlands.* San Francisco: McSweeneys.

Clinton, K. A. (2006). *Being-in-the-digital-world: How videogames engage our prelinguistic sense-making abilities.* (Unpublished doctoral dissertation.) University of Wisconsin–Madison.

Cobb, P., Confrey, J., diSessa, A., Lehrer, R., & Schauble, L. (2003). Design experiments in educational research. *Educational Researcher, 32*(1), 9–13.

Collins, A., & Halverson, R. (2009). *Rethinking education in the age of technology: The digital revolution and schooling in America.* New York: Teachers College Press.

Davidson, C. (2004) [1986]. *Revolution and the word: The rise of the novel in America.* Oxford, UK: Oxford University Press.

Davidson, C. (2008, November 23). Collaboration by difference, yet again. *Humanities, Arts, Science, and Technology Advanced Collaboratory.* Retrieved from http://hastac.org/node/1815

Delandshere, G. (2001). Implicit theories, unexamined assumptions, and the status quo of educational assessment. *Assessment in Education: Principles, Policy, and Practice, 8*(2), 113–133.

Derecho, A. (2006). Archontic literature: A definition, a history, and several theories of fan fiction. In K. Hellekson & K. Busse (Eds.), *Fan fiction and fan communities in the age of the Internet* (pp. 61–78). Jefferson, NC: McFarland.

Donald, M. (1991). *Origins of the modern mind: Three stages in the evolution of culture and cognition.* Cambridge, MA: Harvard University Press.

Donald, M. (1993). Precis of origins of the modern mind: Three stages in the evolution of culture and cognition. *Behavioral and Brain Sciences* 16, 737–791.

Dysthe, O., Engelsen, K. S., & Lima, I. (2007). Variations in portfolio assessment in higher education: Discussion of quality issues based on a Norwegian survey across institutions and disciplines. *Assessing Writing, 12*(2), 129–148.

Eisenstein, E. (1979). *The printing press as an agent of change: Communications and cultural transformations in early modern Europe.* Cambridge, UK: Cambridge University Press.

Elliott, K. (2004). Literary film adaptation and the formal/content dilemma. In M.-L. Ryan (Ed.), *Narrative across media: The languages of storytelling* (pp. 220–243). Lincoln: University of Nebraska Press.

Erickson, F. (1984). School literacy, reasoning, and civility: An anthropologist's perspective. *Review of educational research, 54*(4); 525–546.

Fiske, J. (1994). *Media matters: Race and gender in U.S. politics.* Minneapolis: University of Minnesota Press.

Freire, P. (2009). [1970]. *Pedagogy of the oppressed* (3rd ed.). New York: Continuum.

Gee, J. P. (1992). *The social mind: Language, ideology, and social practice.* New York: Bergin & Garvey.

Gee, J. P. (1998). Review: Ethnography, linguistics, narrative inequality: Toward an understanding of voice. *Language in Society, 27*(2), 247–250.

Gee, J. P. (2003a). Opportunity to learn: A language-based perspective on assessment. *Assessment in Education: Principles, Policy and Practice, 10*(1), 27–46.

Gee, J. P. (2003b). *What videogames have to teach us about learning and literacy.* New York: Palgrave Macmillan.

Gee, J. P. (2004). *Situated language and learning: A critique of traditional schooling.* New York: Routledge.

Gee, J. P. (2009). Human action and social groups as the natural home of assessment: Thoughts on 21st century learning and assessment. In V. J. Shute & B. J. Becker's (Eds.), *Innovative assessment in the 21st century: Supporting educational needs* (pp. 13–40). New York: Springer.

Giroux, H. A. (1991). *Postmodernism, feminism, and cultural politics.* Albany: State University of New York Press.

Green, S., Jenkins, C., & Jenkins, H. (2006). "Normal female interest in men bonking": Selections from the Terra Nostre Underground and Strange Bedfellows. In H. Jenkins' (Ed.), *Fans, bloggers, and gamers: Exploring participatory culture* (pp. 61–88). New York: New York University Press.

Greeno, J. G. (1998). The situativity of knowing, learning, and research. *American Psychologist, 53*(1), 5–26.

Greeno, J. G., & Gresalfi, M. S. (2008). Opportunities to learn in practice and identity. In P. A. Moss, D. C. Pullin, J. P. Gee, E. H. Haertel, & L. Jones Young (Eds.), *Assessment, equity, and opportunity to learn* (pp. 170–199). New York: Cambridge University Press.

Guess, A. (2008, July 8). Cite check. *Inside Higher Ed.* Retrieved from http://insidehighered.com/news/2008/07/08/citation

Habib, L., & Wittek, L. (2007). The portfolio as artifact and actor. *Mind, Culture, and Activity, 14*(4), 266–282.

Hedrick, J. D. (1995). *Harriet Beecher Stowe: A life.* New York: Oxford University Press.

Herrington, A., Hodgson, K., & Moran, C. (2009). Technology, change, and assessment: What we have learned. In A. Herrington, K. Hodgson, & C. Moran (Eds.), *Teaching the new writing: Technology, change, and assessment in the 21st-century classroom* (pp. 198–208). New York: Teachers College Press.

Hickey, D. T. (2011). Participation by design: Improving individual motivation by looking beyond it. In D. M. McInerney, R. A. Walker, & G. A. D. Liem (Eds.), *Sociocultural theories of learning and motivation: Looking back, looking forward* (pp. 137–161). Charlotte, NC: Information Age.

Hickey, D. T., & Anderson, K. T. (2007). Situative approaches to student assessment: Contextualizing evidence to support practice. In *Yearbook of the National Society for the Study of Education: Evidence and Decision Making, 106*(1), 264–287.

Hickey, D. T., Honeyford, M. A., Clinton, K. A., & McWilliams, J. (2010). Participatory assessment of 21st century proficiencies. In V. J. Shute & B. J. Becker (Eds.), *Innovative assessment in the 21st century: Supporting educational needs* (pp. 107–138). New York: Springer.

Hickey, D. T., Ingram-Goble, A., & Jameson, E. M. (2009). Designing assessments and assessing designs in virtual educational environments. *Journal of Science Education and Technology, 18*(2), 187–208.

Hickey, D. T., McWilliams, J., & Honeyford, M. A. (2011). Reading *Moby-Dick* in a participatory culture: Organizing assessment for engagement in a new media era. *Journal of Educational Computing Research, 45*(2), 247–263.

Hickey, D. T., Zuiker, S. J., Taasoobshirazi, G., Schafer, N. J., & Michael, M. A.

(2006). Balancing varied assessment functions to attain systemic validity: Three is the magic number. *Studies in Educational Evaluation, 32*(3), 180–201.

Hobbs, R. (2010). *Copyright clarity: How fair use supports digital learning.* Thousand Oaks, CA: Corwin.

Ison, V. (2010, March 3). Opinion: Aurora students impress a student who doesn't know them. *The Herald-Times.* Retrieved from http://www.heraldtimesonline. com/stories/2010/03/03/digitalcity.qp-6323763.sto

Ita, S. (2007). *Moby-Dick: A pop-up book.* New York: Sterling.

Ito, M., Baumer, S., Bittanti, M., boyd, d., Cody, R., Herr-Stephenson, B., Horst, H. A., Lange, P. G., Mahendran, D., Martinez, K. Z., Pascoe, C. J., Perkel, D., Robinson, L., Sims, C., & Tripp, L. (2010). *Hanging out, messing around, and geeking out: Kids living and learning with new media.* Cambridge, MA: MIT Press/MacArthur Foundation.

Jenkins, H. (1988). *Star Trek* rerun, reread, rewritten: Fan writing as textual poaching. *Critical Studies in Mass Communication, 5*(2), 85–107.

Jenkins, H. (1992). *Textual poachers: Television fans and participatory culture.* New York: Routledge.

Jenkins, H. (2006a). *Convergence culture: Where old and new media collide.* New York: New York University Press.

Jenkins, H. (2006b, August 25). Getting Lost. *Confessions of an Aca-fan.* Retrieved from http://henryjenkins.org/2006/08/getting_lost.html

Jenkins, H. (2007a, January 18). The merits of nitpicking: A doctor diagnoses *House. Confessions of an Aca-Fan.* Retrieved from http://henryjenkins. org/2007/01/the_merits_of_knitpicking_a_do.html

Jenkins, H. (2007b, June 26). What Wikipedia can teach us about the new media literacies (part one). *Confessions of an Aca-Fan.* Retrieved from http://www. henryjenkins.org/2007/06/what_wikipedia_can_teach_us_ab.html

Jenkins, H. (2008a, September 22). Teaching "Ahab": An interview with MC Lars. *Confessions of an Aca-Fan.* Retrieved from http://henryjenkins.org/2008/09/ teaching_ahab_an_interview_wit.html

Jenkins, H. (2008b, June 2). "What is remix culture?": An interview with Owen Gallagher. *Confessions of an Aca-Fan.* Retrieved from http://henryjenkins. org/2008/06/interview_with_total_remixs_ow.html

Jenkins, H., Purushotoma, R., Weigel, M., Clinton, K., & Robison, A J. (2009). *Confronting the challenges of participatory culture: Media education for the 21st century.* Cambridge, MA: MIT Press.

Jenkins, H. (2009, June 8). Multiculturalism, appropriation, and the new media literacies. *Confessions of an Aca-Fan.* Retrieved from http://henryjenkins. org/2009/06/multiculturalism_appropriation.html

Jenkins, H., & Felt, L. (2010, September 1). High tech? Low tech? No tech? *Confessions of an Aca-Fan*. Retrieved from http://henryjenkins.org/2010/09/high_tech_low_tech_no_tech.html

Justin, with Hobb, R. (2005, November 9). In defense of fanfiction: Guest blogger Justin Goes hobbnobbing. *Swifty, writing*. Retrieved from http://swiftywriting.blogspot.com/2005/11/in-defense-of-fanfiction-guestblogger.html

Kelley, W. (2008). *Herman Melville: An introduction*. Oxford, UK: Wiley-Blackwell.

Kozol, J. (1991). *Savage inequalities: Children in America's schools*. New York: Crown.

Lankshear, C., & Knobel, M. (2007). Sampling "the new" in new literacies. In M. Knobel & C. Lankshear (Eds.), *A new literacies sampler* (pp. 1–24). New York: Peter Lang.

Lauter, P. (1994). Melville climbs the canon. *American Literature, 66*(1), 1–24.

Lenhart, A., & Madden, M. (2005). *Teen content creators and consumers*. Pew Internet and American Life Project. Retrieved from http://www.pewinternet.org/PPF/r/166/report_display.asp

Lenhart, A., Purcell, K., Smith, A., & Zickuhr, K. (2010). *Social media and mobile Internet use among teens and young adults*. Pew Internet and American Life Project. Retrieved from http://pewresearch.org/pubs/1484/social-media-mobile-internet-use-teens-millennials-fewer-blog

Lévy, P. (1997). *Collective intelligence: Mankind's emerging world in cyberspace*. Cambridge, MA: Perseus Books.

Long, G. (1833–1843). *Penny cyclopaedia of the society for the diffusion of useful knowledge*. London, UK: Charles Knight.

Lord, A. E. (2000). *The singer of tales*. Cambridge, MA: Harvard University Press.

Lund, A., & Rasmussen, I. (2010). Tasks 2.0: Education meets social computing and mass collaboration. In D. Gibson & B. Dodge (Eds.), *Proceedings of Society for Information Technology and Teacher Education International Conference 2010* (pp. 4058–4065). Chesapeake, VA: Association for the Advancement of Computing in Education.

Maier, S. F., & Seligman, M. E. P. (1976). Learned helplessness: Theory and evidence. *Journal of Experimental Psychology: General, 105*(1), 3–46.

Malnassy, L. K. (2002). "The Bizarre Breasts Tutorial: How to Draw Breasts," *Sequential Tart*, July, http://www.sequentialtart.com/archive/july02/bb_0702.shtml

MC Lars. (2006, October 24). *Ahab*. YouTube. Retrieved from http://www.youtube.com/watch?v=ZW76mvaaXEc

McDonald, J. (2003). *Twists and turns*. New York: Farrar, Strauss and Giroux.

McGrath, C. (2007, January 7). Plagiarism: Everyone into the pool. *New York Times*. Retrieved from http://www.nytimes.com/2007/01/07/education/edlife/07books.html

Melville, H. (2007). J. Bryant and H. Springer (Eds.), *Moby-Dick*. New York: Pearson Education.

Moore, J. A., & Barab, S. (2002). The inquiry learning forum. *TechTrends, 46*(3), 44–49.

Morrison, T. (1992). *Playing in the dark*. New York: Vintage.

New Media Literacies. (2008). *Expert Vvoices: A Ssupplement to the TSG*. Retrieved from http://newmedialiteracies.org/ExpertVoices_Revised.pdf

O'Brien, T. (1990). *The things they carried*. New York: Broadway.

Olsen-Smith, S., Marnon, D., & Norberg, P. (Eds.). (n.d.). *Melville's marginalia online*. Retrieved from http://melvillesmarginalia.org/

Ong, W. (2002). *Orality and literacy*. New York: Routledge.

Popham, W. J. (1997). What's wrong—and what's right—with rubrics. *Educational Leadership, 55*(2), 72–75.

Pugh, S. (2006). *The democratic genre: Fan fiction in a literary context*. London, UK: Seren.

Rabinowitz, P. J. (1985). The turn of the glass key: Popular fiction as reading strategy. *Critical Inquiry, 11*(3), 418–431.

Renker, E. (2007). *The origins of American literature studies: An institutional history*. New York: Cambridge University Press.

Rideout, V. J., Foehr, U. G., & Roberts, D. F. (2010). *Generation M2: Media in the lives of 8- to 18-year olds*. Menlo Park, CA: Kaiser Family Foundation. Retrieved from http://www.kff.org/entmedia/upload/8010.pdf

Rodriguez, D. (2007). *Kabul Beauty School: An American woman goes behind the veil*. New York: Random House.

Shaffer, D. W., & Kaput, J. J. (1999). Mathematics and virtual culture: An evolutionary perspective on technology and mathematics education. *Educational Studies in Mathematics, 37*, 97–119.

Shaffer, D. W., Squire, K. D., Halverson, R., & Gee, J. P. (2005). Video games and the future of learning. *Phi Delta Kappan, 87*(2), 104–111.

Shepard, L. A. (2007). Formative assessment: Caveat emptor. In C. A. Dwyer (Ed.), *The future of assessment: Shaping teaching and learning* (pp. 279–303). Mahwah, NJ: Lawrence Erlbaum Associates.

Shirky, C. (2008a). "Gin, television, and social surplus." Web 2.0 Expo. SF. Retrieved from http://blip.tv/web2expo/web-2-0-expo-sf-2008-clay-shirky-862384

Shirky, C. (2008b). *Here comes everybody: The power of organizing without organizations.* New York: Penguin.

Sigler, C. (1997). *Alternative Alices: Visions and revisions of Lewis Carroll's Alice books.* Lexington: University Press of Kentucky.

Stallybrass, P. (2002). Books and scrolls: Navigating the Bible. In J. Anderson & E. Sauer's (Eds.), *Books and readers in early modern England: Material studies* (pp. 42–79). Philadelphia: Pennsylvania University Press.

Stowe, H. B. (1999) [1859]. *The minister's wooing.* New York: Penguin Books.

Taasoobshirazi, G., Zuiker, S. J., Anderson, K. T., & Hickey, D. T. (2006). Enhancing inquiry, understanding, and achievement in an astronomy multimedia learning environment. *Journal of Science Education and Technology, 15*(5), 383–395.

Tapscott, D. (2009). *Grown up digital: How the Net generation is changing the world.* New York: McGraw-Hill.

Tulloch, J., & Jenkins, H. (1995). *Science fiction audiences: Watching* Star Trek *and* Doctor Who. London, UK: Routledge.

Uricchio, W., & Pearson, R. (1993). *Reframing culture: The case of the Vitagraph Quality Films.* Trenton, NJ: Princeton University Press.

Yancey, K. B. (2009). *Writing in the 21st century: A report from the National Council of Teachers of English.* Urbana, IL: National Council of Teachers of English. Retrieved from http://www.ncte.org/library/NCTEFiles/Press/Yancey_final.pdf

Zeleny, J. (2008, February 19). Clinton camp says Obama plagiarized in speech. *New York Times.* Retrieved from http://www.nytimes.com/2008/02/19/us/politics/19campaign.html

Index

About the Editors
and Contributors

Editors

Henry Jenkins, the Provost's Professor of communications, journalism, cinematic arts, and education at the University of Southern California, is the editor or author of 14 books on various aspects of media and popular culture, including *Textual Poachers: Television Fans and Participatory Culture, From Barbie to Mortal Kombat: Gender and Computer Games* (with Justine Cassell), *Convergence Culture: Where Old and New Media Collide*, and *Spreadable Media: Creating Meaning and Value in a Networked Culture* (with Sam Ford and Joshua Green).

Wyn Kelley, senior lecturer in literature and comparative media studies at the Massachusetts Institute of Technology, is author of *Melville's City: Literary and Urban Form in Nineteenth-Century New York* (1996) and *Herman Melville: An Introduction* (2008).

Katie Clinton earned her PhD in curriculum and instruction at the University of Wisconsin–Madison and is currently affiliated with New Media Literacies at the University of Southern California. She is a co-author of *Confronting the Challenges of Participatory Culture: Media Education for the 21st Century*.

Jenna McWilliams is a doctoral student in the learning sciences at Indiana University, where her current work focuses on equity, culturally relevant pedagogy, and queer and critical theory. Previously, McWilliams worked at New Media Literacies as a researcher and curriculum specialist.

Ricardo Pitts-Wiley is the co-founder along with his wife, Bernadet, of Mixed Magic Theatre in Pawtucket, Rhode Island. Since 2005 Pitts-Wiley has devoted most of his time to teaching and adapting works of literature for the stage. To date he has created works based on *Moby-Dick*, the poems of Paul Laurence Dunbar, *Don Quixote, Frankenstein, The Red Tent,* and the *Narrative of the Life of Frederick Douglass.* He has taught acting and directed plays at MIT, the University of Rhode Island, Southhampton College—Long Island University, and Salve Regina University.

Erin Reilly is managing director for Annenberg Innovation Lab and research director for New Media Literacies at the University of Southern California's Annenberg School for Communications and Journalism. Having received multiple awards, such as Cable in a Classroom's Leaders in Learning, her current projects include the PLAY! platform, a transmedia learning playground for the curation, creation, and circulation of user-generated learning activities that cultivates co-learning among adults and youth, and Flotsam's Transmedia Experience, an exploration of collective storytelling.

Contributors

Rudy "Rudacious" Cabrera was an actor in *Moby-Dick: Then and Now* when it was produced by the Mixed Magic Theatre in Pawtucket, Rhode Island.

Daniel T. Hickey is an associate professor in the learning sciences program at Indiana University in Bloomington and a research professor with the Indiana University Center for Research on Learning and Technology. He has directed projects focused on participatory approaches to assessment, feedback, evaluation, and motivation and technology-supported learning environments funded by the National Science Foundation, NASA, and the MacArthur Foundation.

Michelle Honeyford is an assistant professor in language and literacy in the Faculty of Education at the University of Manitoba. A former English language arts teacher and research associate at Rockman et al, she has conducted research on programs funded by the U.S. Department of Education,

National Endowment for the Arts, Poetry Foundation, National Science Foundation, and MacArthur Foundation.

Hillary Kolos is currently the director of digital learning at DreamYard, the largest arts education provider in the Bronx, New York. As a graduate student in the comparative media studies program at MIT, she worked as a research assistant for New Media Literacies and researched gaming culture.

Judith Nirenberg is the librarian at Somerville High School in Somerville, Massachusetts. She has taught at all age levels, and her experience has included teaching anthropology to nurses at Northeastern University in Boston.

Rebecca Rupert is a 9th- and 10th-grade language arts teacher at Monroe County Community School Corporation in Bloomington, Indiana; a Hoosier Writing Project teacher consultant; and a National Board certified teacher.